WRITE AWAY

WRITE AWAY

A Year of Musings and Motivations for Writers

By Kerrie Flanagan

&

Jenny Sundstedt

For Granny's Library,
Wishing you inspiration
+ creativity !!

Denie

Printed in the United States of America
First Printing, 2014
Hot Chocolate Press
Fort Collins, Colorado

http://HotChocolatePress.com

Cover design by: Ania Cywińska

ISBN: **978-0-9910626-4-5**

www.KerrieFlanagan.com

This book is dedicated to all the writers in our lives: past, present, and future.

ACKNOWLEDGMENTS

From Kerrie:

The African proverb says it takes a village to raise a child and I think the same idea can be applied to the publishing of a book; it also takes a village. Without the love and support of my husband, Rich, and the rest of my family I would not be a writer and this book would have only been a fleeting thought.

I also want to thank my co-author, Jenny Sundstedt, a talented writer who makes me laugh and inspires me to find the humor in everyday situations. I look forward to creating more books with her in the future.

And finally, I'd like to thank Writer's Group. These amazing, gifted writers always encourage me to be the best writer I can be. Over the years we have shared our writing, celebrated each other's successes, laughed until we cried, grieved the losses of loved ones and supported each other with our writing and with life. I look forward to many more years together, Ellen, LeAnn, Linda, Helen, Carol and Kelly.

From Jenny:

Thanks so much to my family and friends who enthusiastically support me in all my writing endeavors (even when there is no tangible evidence that such endeavors are actually taking place):

- My husband and best friend, Mark; my sons, Nathan and David; my mother, Sara; and my sister, Amy—also known as the best family ever. Your wisdom and encouragement mean the world to me;

- The members of Northern Colorado Writers, including amazing creative team partners April and Kelly;

- The Writing Bug's readers and fellow bloggers;

- Dodi and Janell, for the hours of talking and walking that keep me sane;

- And especially my co-author Kerrie, without whom Northern Colorado Writers, and this book, would not exist.

I appreciate you all and hope to someday invite you to a party on my private island, where Stephen King and James Patterson will serve us tropical drinks from silver trays. (Disclaimer: I do not currently own any part of an island, private or otherwise, and Mr. King and Mr. Patterson have in no way, shape, or form agreed to bartending services of any kind.)

HOW TO USE THIS BOOK

This book, created by and for writers, combines humorous and insightful stories with tips, tools, and interactive elements to help writers reflect on where they are at the moment and plan where they want to be in the future.

Each month begins with goal setting and creating the action steps to achieving those goals. Goals are like a GPS for our brain. They give our brain a direction, something to work toward. When we don't set goals, we can feel lost and frustrated.

To make goal setting easier and more effective:

- Write them down
- Be specific and positive
- Set deadlines for achieving your goals
- Be as detailed as possible
- Say what you will or intend to do

Start with a few big goals for the year (e.g., "I will find a literary agent for my middle-grade novel by December"). Write the goals down and post them in a place you will see them every day.

Each month, create a couple of smaller goals related to those (e.g., "Find eight agents to query"). Write the goals in the space provided. (If you are reading this as an ebook, you can visit the Hot Chocolate Press website to download those pages). Then write down the action steps you will take to achieve those (e.g., "I will spend one hour each week researching potential agents").

The idea is that all of your actions reflect your bigger goals, keeping you focused and on track.

Visualize

Picture yourself achieving your goals. Imagine getting the call from the agent or seeing your article in that national magazine or holding your newly published book.

Share

Find a writing buddy. Share your goals with each other and provide encouragement and support along the way. Having someone to hold you accountable helps you stay on track.

Reward

Be sure to reward yourself when you have accomplished your goal/s for the month.

As additional motivation, questions and exercises are woven throughout the book. Take the time to reflect on the questions. Don't be afraid to write in the book in the spaces we left blank or in a special journal. The exercises are there to help you focus on various aspects of your writing and will be helpful at different times on your writing journey.

The section in the back of the book has cures for writers block, resources, and tools to help you along the way. There is even a section where you can track submissions you send out.

The book is divided into twelve months. It begins in January, but it can be picked up at any time of year and can be used for years to come.

Happy Writing!

—Kerrie & Jenny

This page intentionally left blank for Notes and Doodles

CONTENTS

JANUARY

"A professional writer is an
amateur who didn't quit."
—*Richard Bach*

Writing Goals for the Month

_____
_____
_____
_____
_____

Action Steps to Achieve Your Goals

_____
_____
_____
_____
_____

Reward

_____

WORD FOR THE YEAR

-Kerrie

At my writers group last week we talked about our writing goals for the next year. One member boldly stated that she doesn't have any. Instead, she creates a word (or theme) for the year.

Her word for the New Year was **Connect**. She planned to grow her freelance and website business, so to do that, she intended to focus on connecting with other people and businesses.

We all loved this idea of a word for the year, so we switched our focus from goals to thinking about our own words. One member chose the word **Finish**. She had many unfinished projects vying for her attention, and she wanted to complete them. Another member declared **Try** as his word. He planned to try to get an agent or publisher for his book and keep trying to get his short stories and essays published.

I declared **Dream** as my word. I like to think big, and this year I have some big dreams for my own writing and for my writing organization, Northern Colorado Writers.

What is your word for the year?

Post this word somewhere you will see it every day. Get creative with colors and designs. Make it something you enjoy looking at each day.

6 IMPOSSIBLE THINGS
-Jenny

It's the New Year, and the blogosphere is teeming with resolutions. Last year, so much—well, let's call it "debris"—hit the fan that we're all ready for a clean, fresh start. And I think this national January pastime of resolution-making is particularly compelling for writers. Starting a new project, completing an old one, editing, querying, classes, conferences—we have no shortage of goal-worthy pursuits.

I usually make resolutions. This year, however, I'm trying something different, inspired by Tim Burton's reimagining of *Alice in Wonderland*. Early in the movie, when Alice remarks to her stick-in-the-mud potential fiancé that she wonders what it would be like to fly, he asks her why she would spend time thinking of such an impossible thing. She can't imagine why she *wouldn't* and tells him that her late father sometimes believed in six impossible things even before breakfast.

Near the end of the movie, as Alice battles the ferocious Jabberwocky, she gathers her courage by reminding herself to believe in six impossible things. "One: there's a potion that can make you shrink.

Two: and a cake that can make you grow. Three: animals can talk. Four: cats can disappear. Five: there's a place called Wonderland. Six: I can slay the Jabberwocky."

She does slay the beast. Then she returns to tell the dull Seamus that she won't marry him. Instead, she embarks on an exciting new business adventure with her father's friend.

Inspired by Alice's moxie, I've decided that instead of making resolutions this year, I will believe in six impossible things every day before breakfast. For example:

1. Chocolate can make me thin;
2. I can win a million dollars just by using my Discover Card;
3. My kitchen can stay clean for longer than five minutes;
4. I can master time management;
5. With the right shampoo, my hair can look like Jennifer Aniston's; and
6. I can vanquish the dreaded slush pile like my own personal Jabberwocky.

My rational mind knows that the odds of these things happening might not be in my favor—and probably a kajillion-to-one for #2—but there's something very liberating about giving myself permission to be open to the idea that anything can happen. As Alice's father says, "The only way to achieve the impossible is to believe it is possible."

What impossible things will you believe in this year?

MOVING BEYOND WANT

-Kerrie

Those who become successful writers are not always the most talented ones, but they are always the ones who did not give up. They pushed through the tough times, they passed those who dropped out, and they made the decision to cross the finish line.

Someone told me that what you *want* becomes irrelevant without a decision. This is so true when it comes to writing. I come across people all the time who say they *want* to be writers. They talk about all the things they *want* to write, or all the novels they *want* to finish. But they never do anything about it.

There are so many things I *want*. I want to spend a year in Alaska, I want to see the Northern Lights, I want to attend the Book Expo of America, I want to publish a short story . . . Are all of these things possible for me? Of course they are. I just need to make a decision to stop wanting and to start doing.

Jack Canfield and Mark Victor Hansen created the Chicken Soup for the Soul empire. This would not have happened if they hadn't decided to publish the first *Chicken Soup for the Soul* book. They also decided that NOT publishing it was NOT an option.

So, they persevered. They didn't quit after 20, 50, 100 publishers said no. When someone said "no," Jack and Mark would say, "next." After 123 rejections, Heath Communications gave them the yes they had been waiting for. They have now sold over 100 million *Chicken Soup for the Soul* books.

Is this the year you will move beyond wanting to write and make the decision to actually be a writer? Are you willing to do what it takes to finish that novel, write that article, start that blog, or find an agent? Are you ready to invest time in your writing, have confidence in your abilities, and push through to the finish line? If so, this is going to be a great year for you.

List three things you can do to move from *wanting* to be a writer to *being* a writer

STAYING OUT OF A DITCH
-Jenny

If you're "lucky" enough to live in a part of the world that experiences snow and ice this time of year, you know that they present particular challenges for drivers. Whether braving the interstate or getting going at a four-way stop, traction is a real issue. Slippery roads aside, "traction" is used in other contexts, too. Medically, it is a pulling force exerted on a skeletal structure. In more general terms, "traction" can refer to an idea or project generating sufficient momentum to move forward.

Having gotten new tires last fall, I feel confident in my car's traction this season. Not so with my writing. I can't tell you how many times my writing plans slid off into the ditch last year. If there was such a thing as AAA for writers, I'd be on a first-name basis with the tow truck driver. ("Hey, it's me. My manuscript went flat, and I'm stranded. Yes, again.") So I thought I'd look to some winter driving tips for a little help.

- **Make sure you have the necessary equipment before starting out.** Chocolate, tea, an inspirational book or two, and a few great ideas. Your outline is your road map.
- **Decrease your speed.** Well, I'm a pretty slow writer, but for anyone who zooms from one project to the next, finished or not, try to ease up on the accelerator a bit. Decaf helps.
- **Turn on your lights to increase your visibility.** Visibility? I fly so far under the radar that the Pentagon couldn't find me, let alone an agent.
- **Keep your windshield clean.** It always helps to see where you're going—in driving, in writing, and in life.
- **If you start to slide, steer in the direction of the skid.** When our writing is headed in a direction we hadn't intended, it's natural to want to turn back the other way. But maybe we should go with it and see where it takes us.

- **Use a shovel to clear away snow**—or that giant drift of papers on your desk that prevents you from focusing on your writing.
- **If stuck, don't spin your wheels.** It only makes things worse. Try a quick walk, making soup, a hot shower . . . anything that acts like ice-melt on your brain freeze.

What helps you regain traction when your writing starts to slide?

GET OUT OF YOUR OWN WAY
-Kerrie

After more than a decade of writing nonfiction, I am trying my hand at a novel. I have held off sharing it with my critique group—or anyone, for that matter. I wanted to get far enough along to have a solid understanding of the story line and characters before getting input. When the time came for me to get input from other people, I sent off my first three chapters to a few trusted writing friends for feedback, then anxiously waited for their responses.

They all sent back good/helpful feedback, but one friend, who has known me the longest and has seen my writing from the very beginning, said to me, "You're getting in your own way. You are letting the 'rules' dictate your writing."

A light bulb went off. For the past few years, I have taught classes about "the rules" of writing, and I have worked with other writers on fixing up their manuscripts. I had immersed myself in the rules and now it had gotten the best of me.

Some of the rules in question include
- Get rid of the passives

- "was" is a bad word
- Don't use "-ing" words
- Delete ALL adverbs
- Vary your sentence structure
- Too much description bogs down a story
- Each character should have a distinct voice
- Don't include "info dumps"
- Avoid clichés like the plague

My friend went on to add, "We get so caught up in making it good writing, we forget about making it good reading."

This point became crystal clear when my friend said the chapter that flowed and read really well was the third chapter. I told her that was a chapter I wrote about six years ago when I got the original idea for the book.

Six years ago, I wasn't letting rules dictate my writing. I was writing for the sake of writing and working hard to convey the scene to the best of my ability at the time. I wasn't thinking of the rules or who might be reading it, I was just writing.

Am I saying disregard the rules completely? No, but we shouldn't let them be the guiding force in our writing. We need to let our creative self take the helm and give it the freedom to travel where it needs to go without all the rules getting in the way.

What rules get in your way?

Try writing without them and see what happens.

FEBRUARY

"No tears in the writer, no tears in the reader. No
surprise in the writer, no surprise in the reader."
—*Robert Frost*

Writing Goals for the Month

_____

_____

_____

_____

_____

Action Steps to Achieve Your Goals

_____

_____

_____

_____

_____

Reward

_____

WRITING NAKED

-Jenny

February 1st is Working Naked Day. Didn't have it on your calendar, you say? Me, neither. I ran across it that morning while foraging in the Internet wilderness. According to Founder and Home Office Expert Lisa Kanarek, "Working Naked refers to the fact that when we begin working from home, we're stripped of all of the corporate support that makes up our day-to-day existence." It also means actually working *sans* clothing.

I wondered who would be crazy enough to do it. Upon further reflection, I realized that my work is writing (though it's frustratingly pro bono these days), and I write at home. Maybe I should be crazy enough to give it a try. What the heck, I might learn something about myself in the process.

I gathered my nerve, and, after boys and husband were out the door and the dog was walked, I retreated to the privacy of my basement computer, fired up the space heater, stripped down to my slippers, and committed myself to one hour of nude writing. No joke. I really did.

How did it go? Let's just say it was a looong hour, but I made it through . . . barely (excuse the pun). I wish I could say I felt liberated, enlightened, or even merely silly. But, frankly, it was an uncomfortable experience. And not just because I was freezing. In the spirit of the classic *Seinfeld* episode comparing "good naked" and "bad naked," I confess I am not a fan of casual nudity. If the UPS man is ever going to surprise me in the buff (mine, not his), he's going to have to deliver right to my shower door.

I'm certain that Working Naked Day will not be an annual event for me, but I'm glad I tried it. First of all, I was immune to my normal distractions. I had zero urge to wander up to the kitchen for a snack. The thought of answering the phone made me blush. So, I got a lot of writing done.

It also made me grateful for all the times I don't have to work naked, literally or figuratively. I may not have "corporate support," but I'm so fortunate to have a great network of family and friends, and the wonderful Northern Colorado Writers community.

Last but not least, this experiment encouraged me to consider how much time I spend in my comfort zone. Like many writers, I love my comfort zone. If I, of all people, can work naked for an hour, I can certainly expand my writer's horizons in other small ways. Fully clothed, of course.

What do you do to break out of your comfort zone?

CHARACTERIZATION WITH SOLE
-*Kerrie*

Years ago, I heard a tip from an editor at a workshop. "Describe your character from the feet up," she said. I thought that was an interesting approach. Not long after that workshop, I witnessed this technique in action in a movie, and I was amazed at its effectiveness.

I went to see *The Women*, starring Meg Ryan, Annette Bening, Debra Messing, and Jada Pinkett-Smith. The movie is based on a 1936 Clare Booth Luce play and is the epitome of a chick flick. Women filled the theater—except for the two lone guys who I figured owed their wives/girlfriends big-time.

I enjoyed the movie, but it was the opening credits that I found brilliant. As each star's name flashed across the screen, all we saw of her character was her feet as she walked.

- Annette Bening: Prada's
- Jada Pinkett Smith: Heavy-duty, black leather boots with lots of buckles
- Debra Messing: Flat pumps and she was pushing a stroller
- Meg Ryan: Flats

I was amazed at how much I could tell about the characters before the movie even started, just by knowing what kind of shoes they wore.

Obviously in film we have the benefit of seeing, but I'm sure the screenwriter had to write this scene so the director would understand what was going on.

I think this is important for writers to think about because sometimes we go to great lengths to describe a character's personality when we really don't need to. All we really need to do is put in some other minor descriptions, like shoes, and through those, our character's personality comes through.

Take a few minutes to describe the shoes your main characters wear:

LOVE YOUR WRITING
-Jenny

Love is in the air this month, which brings to mind this quote from Norman Mailer: "(Writing) a novel is more like falling in love (than non-fiction). You don't say, 'I'm going to fall in love next Tuesday, I'm going to begin my novel.' The novel has to come to you. It has to feel just like love." By the same token, novelist Pico Iyer wrote that "Writing should . . . be as spontaneous and urgent as a letter to a lover."

New beginnings, be they with a person or a manuscript, are exciting, full of energy and promise. But as anyone who is fortunate enough to be in a long-term relationship knows, the initial passion changes over time. It mellows and it deepens. It gets comfortable and perhaps even complacent on occasion.

When the thrill of completing the first draft becomes a distant memory, a relationship with a Work in Progress can go the same route. So how does one rekindle a WIP's spark? (Especially if one occasionally fantasizes about feeding a hard copy of one's WIP through the shredder, driving north about sixty miles, and scattering the shreds to the ever-present Wyoming winds?)

How about applying the standard chick-magazine love tips? For example:

Turn up the heat: Give your characters something to get excited about. Romance works, but so does a good argument, or pulse-racing peril. Even if the scene doesn't quite have a place in your WIP, write it anyway, just to see what happens.

Set the mood: Put on some music that fits the tone of your WIP. Adjust the lighting accordingly. Decide what kind of flowers your main character likes and get some for your desk. Cook up some foods your characters would love . . . or hate.

Steal away together: Tell your significant other that you're going to the grocery/shoe/auto parts/pet store. Instead, take your WIP to a quiet place. Sit in a secluded corner. Give your WIP an hour of your undivided attention. Go ahead, whisper a few sweet nothings. No one will hear.

Focus on the positive: Yes, red is the color of romance, but forget the red pen. Instead, get a hot pink highlighter and mark all the passages in your WIP that make you say, "Dang, I *am* a good writer."

Eat chocolate: Various researchers have credited chocolate with improving mood, relaxing blood vessels, boosting circulation, and lowering cholesterol. I say it also fuels creativity and prevents outbreaks of adverbs.

What are three things you love about your WIP today?

DELEGATION, THE KEY TO HAPPINESS AND SUCCESS

-Kerrie

Back in January I won a blog contest. Part of the prize was 30 hours of a virtual assistant through the website TaskUs. This week I finally started cashing in my winnings and had my new assistant do some menial tasks I had been putting off. I now have a detailed spreadsheet of small business grants I can apply for and another spreadsheet of upcoming writers conferences. A new world has opened up for me. It reminded me of the importance of delegating.

I remember reading about delegating in Jack Canfield's book *The Success Principles* and more recently on his blog. He encourages people to focus on their core genius, do what they do well, and delegate the rest.

In theory this is an awesome idea, but for some people, like me, it isn't always easy to implement. Often when I start down the path of finding or hiring someone to help me with tasks, I realize that I will have to explain what needs to be done, and then I second-guess whether they can do it as well as I can (or as well as I think I can). By this time, I usually throw in the towel and do it myself.

The idea that "I can do it all" is not an effective one. I found this out firsthand at my third Northern Colorado Writers Conference. I literally tried to do everything for this conference myself. I did all the marketing, decorating, collecting money, graphic design, picking up people from the airport, making schedules for all the presenters, setting up, making the name tags, taking photos, and being the point person for everything. During the conference I ran around like a crazed madwoman. After the conference I was immobilized for two days.

I vowed to never do that again, and when it comes to the conference, I have followed through with it. Now I have a Creative Team, an Assistant Director, and a crew of volunteer Ambassadors. It has changed the way I approach the whole event. Everything runs much smoother, making it more successful in the long run.

I realized this week with my TaskUs experience that writers should be open to the idea of delegating. Could I have taken the time to compile that information I wanted for the spreadsheets? Of course. But would it have been the best use of my time? I don't think so. Instead of getting hopelessly sucked into the World Wide Web for hours and hours, I used that time to write queries and articles. And isn't that what being a writer is all about— actually writing?

As I think more about it there are probably many tasks I can delegate in order to free up time for writing: research tasks, household chores, blog posts, finding appropriate markets/agents, and updating my website.

By delegating, we can spend more time on our writing, which will inevitably lead to more success.

What are two things you can delegate to free up some writing time?

TAKE A LEAP

-Jenny

Poor February. It's the little brother of the calendar, never quite matching up to the longer months. But every four years, it puffs up its chest a bit with the addition of an extra day. I love the novelty of Leap Day, even though it occasionally gyps me out of a coveted Friday or Saturday birthday.

February 29 is a bonus day, but, as such, how should one choose to spend it? Is it a *do whatever you want because nothing counts day* (i.e., whatever happens on Leap Day stays on Leap Day), or is it a day to take a real shot at something meaningful? Or maybe a little bit of both.

We're told how to celebrate most holidays, whether it's with candy and flowers, fireworks, or green beer. But I say that Leap Day should be celebrator's choice. So, writer friends, it's up to you. If you've been working so hard on a manuscript that you're revising it in your sleep, perhaps your Leap Day should be spent with crossword puzzles and a bottomless cup of tea, or a double feature of completely mindless entertainment at your local movieplex. Cheesecake for lunch is also a viable option.

But if your writerly self has lately been feeling hampered by self-doubts, intimidated by the prospect of success and/or failure, and generally reluctant to strike off in any direction, then perhaps February 29 is your day to take a leap of faith. Send a query. Enter a contest. Register for a conference or sign up for a pitch session. Write a first word, a first line, a first page, a first chapter. You may like it so much that you'll want to treat every day like it's Leap Day. Except for the cheesecake for lunch part.

My leap is sending off one of the short stories I've been sitting on for a while.

What will your writer's leap be?

A GOOD BOOK VS.
A GREAT BOOK
-Kerrie

A few years back on a vacation to Alaska, I became fascinated (obsessed, really) with Matryoshka (nesting) dolls. I loved not knowing how many little wooden dolls I would find hidden inside. It became my quest to find the one around 6 inches tall that had the most in it.

I searched in every store we visited. There was no way to tell from the outside of the doll how many were on the inside. So I opened and opened and opened — each time with great anticipation, each time being a little disappointed when it stopped at five. Then I had to put it back together and try again.

I almost became resigned to the fact that five was as far as any of them would go, but another one caught my eye. It was black with a prince on a white horse painted on it. It reminded me of a fairy tale. I took a deep breath and opened the first one, then the second, all the way to number five.

I suppressed the urge to jump up and scream when I realized I could keep going. I opened the next and the next until I came to number ten, which was about the size of a pencil tip. I yelled to my husband to come and look. I was thrilled. My quest was complete. I went over to the counter and bought it right away.

The other day I was in my living room after reading a disappointing book by a best-selling author. I looked over at my two Matryoshka dolls on the shelf and realized the similarities between my nesting doll quest and the search for a good book.

I like my doll that only has five, but it is not my favorite. My favorite is the one with ten in it, because it goes deeper. Someone took the time to paint the tiny, unique details on each one and to go as far as they could with this set.

My favorite books are the same way. The author has taken the time to create a plot that goes deep and gets to the core of the story. There is complexity in the characters, and I become entrenched in the story. Reading a great book conjures up the same feelings I had when I found my perfect nesting doll. The anticipation built as I revealed each new doll, and the same thing happens with a good book. The author keeps the tension building with one more little "doll" after another, until finally you get to the end, the last "doll." It gives the reader a feeling of great satisfaction—and an urge to track down the author, give him/her a big hug, and say thank you.

As you go back and reread/rework your own novel, short story, or children's book, think about this: Does your story stop at five dolls or does it go into more depth with ten? A five-doll story can be nice—but a ten-doll story is amazing. What kind of story do you want to write?

My quest continues for more ten-doll Matryoshka dolls . . . and for more ten-doll books.

Think about your current Works in Progress (a novel, short story, poem, article . . .). Would you rate them a five-doll or a ten-doll?

How can you add more dolls?

MARCH

"Don't tell me the moon is shining;
show me the glint of light on broken glass."
—*Anton Chekhov*

Writing Goals for the Month

_____

_____

_____

_____

_____

Action Steps to Achieve Your Goals

_____

_____

_____

_____

_____

Reward

_____

AWARDS SEASON

-Jenny

Thanks to my MSN homepage, I know that it is officially awards season. Yes, we have an entire so-called season devoted to recognizing celebrity achievements and critiquing celebrity wardrobes. I'm not much of a Hollywood follower and am always at least a few years behind the rest of the movie-watching world. (How about that Tom Hanks in *Castaway*? Right? Hello?) But I will freely admit that awards season beats West Nile season hands down. Plus, those mosquitoes know nothing about fashion.

In the spirit of awards season, try this: give one of your characters a red-carpet award. Imagine how s/he approaches the podium, what s/he is wearing, how composed s/he is when giving the acceptance speech, whom s/he thanks, whom s/he forgets to thank, how s/he handles it when the music starts playing before s/he is finished. (Or, in a nefarious twist, don't give your character the award and imagine how s/he smiles and applauds, all the while plotting revenge most foul.) Then, for some real fun, follow your character to the after-party.

But maybe your character is too humble for the red carpet and has as little chance of winning an Oscar™ as I have of winning NASA's Most Awesomely Mind-Blowing Rocket Scientist of the Century Award. (I'm pretty sure that's a real thing.) Try giving him or her a blogging award instead. In case you're unfamiliar, they work something like this: *Here's your fun award, fellow blogger! In your acceptance post, tell us seven things we don't know about you. And then pass this award on to 413 other bloggers who do not already have the super-cool badge displayed on the sidebar—and are NOT robots/squirrels/zombies/ genetically engineered dolphins posing as actual blogging people.*

Assuming your character is not a vampire or Galapagos tortoise and therefore has a normal human lifespan, s/he can skip the second part and focus on the list. What will s/he put on that list? Well, we're writers, we can help with that. I'll start with #1: Once swapped tequila shots in an airport bar with Nicholas Cage. As to whether the character is a Navy SEAL or a retired librarian, I'll leave that up to you.

What would you put on your character's list of seven?

IMPRESSING AN AGENT AT A WRITERS CONFERENCE

-Kerrie

As the director of the Northern Colorado Writers Conference, I have the privilege of choosing literary agents to bring in for the event. I always have some time set aside to visit with them outside the hustle and bustle of the conference, and I always walk away with a tremendous amount of valuable information. Here are some highlights of things I have learned.

Strong Voice
All agents are looking for writing with a strong voice. Just like our speaking voice, our writing voice distinguishes us from others. Think about Tom

Clancy, Maya Angelou, and Dave Barry. Do you think you would be able to identify their work, even if their name was not on it? Of course. They each have a definitive voice. This is what you want. You want your voice, not someone else's, to shine through in all your writing.

Be Prepared

If you are pitching to an agent/editor at a conference, you need to do your homework. Find out the types of books they each represent, and don't waste their time pitching to them if you know your project isn't a good fit. Just as you are hoping to find an agent or editor, they are hoping to find new authors to represent. If you are pitching a nonfiction book, you should have the book proposal and at least three chapters complete so if they ask you to send it, you are ready to go. If you are pitching fiction, your book needs to be complete before you pitch.

To quote Kristin Nelson, writers with "ideas" for a great novel are a dime a dozen. It's that one in a hundred writer who actually has the perseverance and stamina to sit down and write the entire thing (which is a huge achievement all in itself since the majority of aspiring writers never even make it that far).

Start with the Action

A good hook is imperative. For novels, start with action to get the reader right into the story. Developing the characters for the first few pages is not going to catch the attention of anyone. It is the same thing for query letters. Use a good hook to catch the editor's/agent's attention right from the beginning.

As writers, it is difficult for us to let go of parts of our writing, but the truth is, if a paragraph, page, even a chapter does nothing to move the story along, then it needs to be taken out—no matter how well it is written.

Professionalism Counts

Believe it or not, the agents/editors do care how you look—not whether you have blond hair, smooth skin, or a bleached white smile, but what you wear. One agent told me that she wished writers would dress more professionally. She didn't necessarily want to see business suits, but she wanted to see clean-cut, professional attire. For her, that set the tone and let her know that you understand that this is a business and you are serious about being a professional writer.

Work Ethic

Agents and editors all want to work with authors who have a good, strong work ethic and are easy to work with. They don't want high-maintenance writers. Each editor/agent has a horror story about an author who was demanding and difficult. They did not keep those clients for very long. Keep in mind that agents and editors do talk to one another. If you are difficult to work with, the word will get out, and you may have a hard time finding another agent/editor to represent you.

Likewise, their success depends on the success of their writers, so once they have taken you on as a client, they will work hard to make your project the best it can be.

IT TAKES ALL KINDS

-*Jenny*

The NCW Conference is coming up, and I'm looking forward to a good time with a fun group of writers. One of the great things about writers conferences is how they bring together so many different kinds of people. For example:

- **The Boy/Girl Scout**: Always prepared. Brings entire home office and multiple hard copies of manuscript in a rolling bag.
- **The Minimalist**: Doesn't carry so much as a pencil. Business cards are handwritten sticky notes.
- **The Autobiographer**: Every question during Q&A begins with a personal anecdote.
- **The Chameleon**: Blends silently into all settings. Only visible when blinking.
- **The Shadow**: Accompanies favorite author/industry professional everywhere. Even the restroom.
- **The "We're not worthy!" Wayne and/or Garth**: Observes any and all authors/industry professionals from a comfortable distance.

- **The Hummingbird**: Can't stay put. Sits in on at least part of every session.
- **The Tortoise**: Comes in five minutes late. Always.
- **The Teflon Skillet**: Rejection slides right off. Hey, it's not personal, right?
- **The Cardiologist**: Takes everything to heart.
- **The Cinderella**: Leaves early on Friday. Wonders what everyone is talking about the next morning.
- **The Life of the Party**: No Saturday breakfast, please, just coffee. Lots of coffee.
- **The Nolan Ryan**: Delivers a pitch so fast and flawless, you barely see it coming.
- **The Tim Wakefield**: The pitch is slower, it wobbles all over, but it gets there in the end.

In case you think I'm being overly judgmental, rest assured that I have, at one conference or another, been almost all of the above, sometimes simultaneously. In fact, there are still some personas I have a hard time shaking off (just call me Garth the Chameleon). But I love conferences because I always meet people who inspire me, make me laugh, make me feel welcome among my peers, and, most importantly, make me want to be a better writer.

Do you see yourself on this list?

TIME TO GET RID OF EXCUSES

-*Kerrie*

One of the biggest issues I hear writers bring up is that they find it difficult to find time to write. The bottom line is that if you want to be a serious writer, then you must *make* the time to write. We all have 24 hours in a day, and we all have the power to decide how we are going to use those hours.

If all you can spare is 30 minutes a day, then commit to those 30 minutes. Don't let anything get in your way. Think about it—a half hour a day, five days a week, is two and a half hours a week, which then equals 120 hours a year. That is definitely enough time to make a dent in your novel or write a dozen poems or a few stories or a picture book or two or a dozen articles . . . you get the idea.

Here are some quick tips to help you find success in organizing your time.

- Make a daily/weekly goal for the number of hours you are going to write.
- Schedule your writing times and mark those times on your calendar.
- Stick to your commitment. If someone calls to try to schedule something during your writing time, nicely say to them, "That time won't work for me, I have a prior commitment." No further explanation is necessary.
- Reward yourself after one month of sticking to your plan.

What is one way you can be better about honoring your writing time?

No More Rejections!

-Kerrie

Rejection.

It is such a harsh word. It is definite, direct, and always seen as negative. When I think of rejection, I think of someone being left at the altar, a child being ignored by her parents, or a guy asking a girl to dance and she laughs in his face. That to me is rejection.

Yet as writers, we throw the word around like a ball and even wear it as a badge of honor.

I want to know when a "no thank you" from an editor, agent, or publisher became synonymous with rejection. I don't see them as the same thing at all.

Imagine you are at a nice restaurant and the waiter asks if you are interested in ordering the chef's special: chicken breast stuffed with blanched fresh spinach leaves and Boursin cheese, sautéed shiitake mushrooms, and baked asparagus with balsamic butter sauce. You think it sounds good, but you planned on getting salmon, so you say, "no thank you."

When the waiter goes in the kitchen to put the order in and the chef finds out you ordered something besides her special, do you think she screams and drops to her knees, sobbing, wondering what she did wrong and agonizing over the fact that you didn't want what she was offering?

I don't think so. It boils down to the fact that you were offered something you didn't want, so you responded politely with a "no thank you." It wasn't anything personal. You just didn't feel like eating chicken.

Isn't that the same thing that happens in publishing? We send our work out to see if an agent, editor, or publisher is interested, and they respond with a "yes" or a "no thank you."

They are not rejecting us or our work, they are simply responding to us. They know what they want, and not everyone is going to offer them what they are looking for. Rejection can beat us down, but a response is just that—a response. There is no judgment attached to it, making it easy to move on. It is much easier to tell our critique group, "I got a response from an editor today . . ."

I say we start a movement or even a revolution to stop writers from using the word rejection! Let's call it like it is (a response) and stop being martyrs for the sake of our art.

APRIL

"You have to have confidence in your ability, and
then be tough enough to follow through."
—*Rosalynn Carter*

Writing Goals for the Month

_____

_____

_____

_____

_____

Action Steps to Achieve Your Goals

_____

_____

_____

_____

_____

Reward

_____

LISTEN TO YOUR CHARACTERS

-*Kerrie*

I had the privilege of hearing three of my favorite local authors—Laura Resau, Todd Mitchell, and Amy Kathleen Ryan—speak at Barnes and Noble. Each has a YA book nominated for a Colorado Book Award.

They were there to talk about their writing, but we were also treated to stories about Laura's travels, Todd's crazy teenage years, and Amy's ghostly roommate.

Since 90 percent of my writing is nonfiction and creative nonfiction, I am always fascinated with how fiction writers can crank out a whole novel. A lot of the conversation revolved around characters and how to be a good listener.

Todd shared that it took him five years to write *Secret to Lying*. He said his problem was he kept getting in his own way until he realized that he had to give up the story he wanted to tell and instead listen to the story his main character James wanted to tell. Once he was able to do that, Todd found that the novel came together.

Laura said that there is a small part of her in all her main characters, but they eventually evolve into their own form. She also believes in listening to your characters. She said she has conversations with them in order to better understand who they are and what makes them tick. This provides depth to her characters, making them more relatable to her readers.

Amy unconsciously bases her characters on real people. She said that she finds if she tries to control her characters too much she gets bored. She wants her characters to lead her as she writes.

How about you? Do you listen to your characters?

HELP YOUR GARDEN GROW

-*Kerrie*

Earth Day rolls around every April 22 and causes "green" thoughts to sprout in my mind. On the 40th anniversary of this annual event, we partnered with another family on our cul-de-sac and started what we called our NSA or neighborhood supported agriculture. Together we grew and tended a variety of gardens.

Because of our south-facing yard, most of the vegetables were grown in our garden. With the help of a sod cutter, we cleared away a 20' x 20' section of grass, adding a third section to our existing plots, in addition to the neighbors' small garden beds.

Our plan was to grow tomatoes, a variety of peppers, onions, cauliflower, broccoli, potatoes, zucchini, squash, pumpkins, basil, lettuce, spinach, peas, green beans, carrots, and cabbage.

Around Earth Day, the seeds were already emerging in their tiny pots under the grow lights and near a sunny window.

These baby seeds demanded a lot of attention. They needed to be watered every day, given light for nutrients, and kept safe.

One morning as I checked on my little green infants, I thought of the similarities between tending the garden and tending our writing.

To have a successful garden, we need to devote time to it every day, nurture it, clear the weeds, and provide it with the proper nutrients.

To be a successful writer you need to apply the same principles to your writing life.

Write Every Day

The only way to get better at something is to practice. Writing is no different. If you want to improve your writing, you need to devote time to it every day. Even if you can only spare 15 minutes a day, this adds up and will help you become a better writer.

Nurture Your Creativity

When not nurtured, creativity will begin to fade. It is important to find ways to keep that part of you alive and well. Join a critique group or find a writing buddy. Talking about writing with others who understand it keeps you motivated and inspired.

Get Rid of the Weeds

Nothing is perfect. All writing has weeds. Writers have to be diligent in taking the time to go back through their work to clear out those unwanted passive verbs, adverbs, "thats," "justs," . . .

Provide Nutrients

Like gardens, writers need nutrients. We can find ours by learning more about our craft. Through books, magazines, workshops, and conferences, we can deepen our understanding of the components of good writing and implement those into our own work.

What do you do to tend to yourself as a writer?

BRANCHING OUT

-Jenny

April is a busy month. Yard work suddenly needs doing (why are weeds the first things to sprout?); school projects, sports, and performances kick into high gear; and people like me suddenly realize that there are only two months left for burning through the to-do list before summer vacation hits.

But that's no reason to neglect your writing. After all, nature branches out in all kinds of wild and woolly ways in April, so why shouldn't we? It's a great time to try something new. For example, this is National Humor Month and National Poetry Month. If you've not tried your hand at either of those, maybe now's the time. You could even get all E. C. Bentley about it and combine the two. Edmund Clerihew Bentley was an English humorist who invented the *clerihew*, a form of humorous biographical verse. Yeah, that's right. Take that Mr. Alex Smartypants Trebek. (I confess, I had to look it up.)

When you need a break from weed-pulling, read something from outside your genre while you put up your feet. Or check in with the Blogging from A to Z Challenge. Even if you're not participating, it's a great opportunity to surf a tidal wave of clever, poignant, and fantastically alphabetical blog posts. There are so many dedicated writers out there giving it their all . . . especially on days Q, X, and Z.

April is also the month for many daily observances to inspire writers: Scrabble Day, Look up at the Sky Day, Reach as High as You Can Day, National Librarian Day, Newspaper Columnists Day, Take a Chance Day, Name Yourself Day (for the perfect *nom de plume* perhaps), Tell a Story Day, and Great Poetry Reading Day.

And, because some days are just like that, there's also Blah, Blah, Blah Day and Rubber Eraser Day.

Finally, if you plan to attend a writers conference this month, sit in on a session that wouldn't normally be your first choice. You might learn something that will set you off in a new direction.

How will you branch out with your writing this month?

KNOW YOUR MARKETS
-*Kerrie*

Years ago when I was starting out as a new writer, I attended lots of workshops and conferences, read tons of books, subscribed to magazines, and talked to writers. One thing kept coming up over and over again: Know Your Market. This piece of advice enabled me to find writing successes early on in my career, and it will do the same for you.

It doesn't matter whether you write fiction, nonfiction, magazines, poetry, short stories, business writing—the advice is still the same. A little extra time spent researching the perfect fit for your work will save you time and disappointment in the end.

Some tips apply to any genre:

Read the Guidelines
The Internet makes this so easy. Whether it is a book publisher, a literary agency, or a magazine, the writers' guidelines can be found online. Or get the *Writer's Market* or another book that contains writers' guidelines.

Read What You Want to Write

If you write for magazines, read magazines. If you write young adult books, read YA books. If you write poetry, read poetry . . . I think you get the idea. You must be familiar with the genre you want to write for.

Know the Trends

Understand what is selling or what is popular for your market. For books, notice the titles of best-selling books. Are they long? Short? Descriptive? Vague? It doesn't mean you should change the focus of your book or give up because your genre is not the "hot" genre. Trends always change. You just need to be aware of them.

Advertising (for magazine writers)

Pay attention to the ads in the magazines you write for. What is the age of the people in the ads? What activities are they doing? What products are being highlighted? This will let you know more about the reader of this magazine and give you a better idea how to slant your article.

How well do you know the markets you write for?

JOURNEY TO CHANGE
-Kerrie

To say I was a Journey fan growing up is putting it mildly. From the very first Journey concert I went to at age 13, I was hooked. What started out as mild fascination soon became an obsession. I learned the words to all their songs, bought every teen magazine that mentioned them, taped radio interviews to listen to over and over, went to more of their concerts, joined the Journey fan club, learned to play their songs on the piano, blasted their music from my room every morning while I got ready for school, and hung up posters all over my room.

By the time I finished junior high, every inch of wall space was covered with something Journey related (and I am not kidding or exaggerating when I say every inch was covered. You can ask my mom).

I also fell head over heels in love with lead singer Steve Perry. I swore someday I was going to marry him and be Mrs. Kerrie Perry. I watched MTV (when it actually had music videos) as much as possible in the hopes of getting a glimpse of him.

I was comforted knowing Journey would always be there for me. That was until the unthinkable happened the year I graduated from high school: Steve Perry left Journey.

I was in shock, unprepared for this change. And to top it off, the rest of the band planned to keep moving forward as Journey. For me, Steve Perry and Journey were one and the same. You couldn't have one without the other.

I grieved the loss, continued to listen to their music, and although heartbroken over this change, eventually moved on with my life. When I went off to college I met my real future husband (who some might argue looks a little like my favorite lead singer), got married, and had a couple of kids.

Journey moved on too. After a few years off, they got a new lead singer named Steve. He was okay, but Steve Perry he was not. In my mind my favorite band was a thing of the past. I had finally accepted they were gone.

Five years ago, I was in Walmart in the electronics department. I heard Journey. Old Journey. Steve Perry Journey. I stopped in my tracks and turned toward the wall of televisions. I did a double take. There, on the screens, was an Asian-looking singer, who sounded just like Steve Perry. And although Journey always says "don't stop believing," I couldn't believe what I was seeing.

Turns out this guy, Arnel Pineda from the Philippines, was the new lead singer for Journey. When Steve #2 left the band, the band turned to YouTube to see if they could find a replacement. After almost giving up, they found Arnel.

Even though this new guy sounded just like Steve Perry, I couldn't accept this change. This was not how it used to be, so in my mind, it was not good. I continued to ignore Arnel Journey. I was *faithfully* a Steve Perry Journey fan, and I was sticking to that. But even without my support, Journey's popularity rose, and a new generation of teenagers became fans.

Recently, Arnel Journey came to the area for a concert. People asked if I was going and of course I said no. I was still holding on to my allegiance to Steve Perry, refusing to accept this new change.

One day my brother asked if I had seen the new Journey documentary about Arnel, *Don't Stop Believing: Everyman's Journey,* on Netflix. I hadn't.

He said it was good and I should watch it. I finally did and I have to say, I have an incredible amount of respect for Arnel Pineda and his journey to Journey. I know he is a guy, but this is a true Cinderella story. I am in awe of his perseverance and of the band's determination to push through all the challenges.

Change is hard regardless of where it shows up in our lives. Our favorite band falling apart, children going off to college, friends moving away . . .

Change shakes us at our core. We don't like it.

The same thing happens with our writing. We don't like change. We know there is a part in our novel that is slow and doesn't move the story along, but we can't let it go. Or that great intro paragraph we have in an article that adds words but no real depth to what we are trying to convey.

We don't want to change it because what we have is familiar and comfortable. It doesn't mean it's good, it just means we know there is work and growth involved with changing it. We either don't want to do the work or we are scared.

The sooner we can accept that change is a part of life and a necessary part of our writing, we can move forward, do the work, and reap the benefits.

When we hold tight to the familiar and don't embrace change, we get stuck and miss out on some amazing opportunities to grow.

I can assure you, if Arnel Journey comes back to my area, I will be first in line for tickets. It is time to accept this change with *open arms*.

Is there anything you need to change with your writing life or with a current work in progress?

USE THE WRITE WORD

-*Jenny*

The other day at my son's basketball game, I thought I heard the little girl next to me ask her mother for protest pencils. A moment later, I realized she had said *princess* pencils, but I already had the image in my head of hand-lettered posters reading "Occupy Preschool" or "Make Cookies, Not War."

A close-but-not-quite word can lead a reader's mind in an unintended direction, with unintended results. The English language is full of more sticky word traps than any spell- and grammar-check can identify, so every writer should have a trusted reference guide at the ready. The following examples come from my handy *100 Words Almost Everyone Confuses & Misuses* from the editors of the American Heritage Dictionaries.

Homonyms are old news—we've all known about them since elementary school, right?—but they can still be devious. Complement/compliment, stationary/stationery, principal/principle . . . I hope I'm not the only one who has to double check a usage from time to time.

Other words are just similar enough to be confusing. Blatant and flagrant are often interchanged, with the distinction being that blatant "emphasizes failure to conceal the act," and flagrant "emphasizes the serious wrongdoing inherent in the offense." Flaunt means to exhibit ostentatiously; flout means to show contempt for. And how about seasonal and seasonable? The former means of or dependent on a particular season. The latter means in keeping with the time or season; timely. That's a subtle difference, but editors get paid to spot subtle differences. Ditto for wreak and wreck, prescribe and proscribe, uninterested and disinterested . . . and the list goes on.

Then there are the words that are flat-out used incorrectly. Have you ever heard someone claim to peruse quickly? It's difficult to do that, as peruse means to read or examine thoroughly or with great care. Penultimate sounds as though it should mean something even better than ultimate. But, alas, it means next to last, as in the next-to-last step or next-to-last syllable.

So, take care, writers. Make sure you know whether your main character infers or implies, guards the perimeter or parameter, lays down or lies down. It can make all the difference.

Keep a list of the sticky words that trip you up.

NOT WHAT I ENVISIONED
-Kerrie

Earlier I mentioned my NSA (neighborhood supported agriculture) garden that we shared with some neighbors. After all the rain and snow we received early on in the season, the garden finally started thriving.

When we first sowed the seeds and planted the fragile seedlings, I wanted to do something to protect the plants without using pesticides. I read somewhere that marigolds can deter unwanted insects.

I liked this idea. I envisioned a border of cute, 6-inch marigolds all the way around the garden, bursting with yellows and oranges. I happened to have a packet of seeds lying around that I had gotten in a box of cereal. Perfect. I planted the seeds and smiled. This was going to be the best garden ever.

As the summer went on, the garden began to flourish, and the border of marigolds joined in the fun. But instead of stopping at a cute 6-inch height, the marigolds kept growing and growing and growing (and no flowers yet). My husband asked if I was sure I planted marigolds.

"Yes," I insisted. "I'm sure they were."

When they hit about the 2-foot mark, something had to be done. They were starting to shield the peppers and onions from the sun. I wasn't worried about the pumpkins and cucumbers because they are strong, viney plants with an attitude. But I had to save the rest of the veggies. So I pulled out some of the marigolds and replanted them in another section of the yard where they wouldn't bully any small fragile plants. So much for my original garden vision.

Has this ever happened with your writing? You have a vision of where you want your story or article to go, but somewhere along the way, something goes wrong. You take your characters on a bunny trail, or you include unnecessary information, or you put some bizarre twist in the middle of your story that makes no sense.

What did I learn from all this? Things don't always go as planned. And never trust seeds from a cereal box.

What do you do to fix this when it happens?

MAY

"A writer is someone for whom writing is more difficult than it is for other people."
—*Thomas Mann*

Writing Goals for the Month

_____

_____

_____

_____

_____

Action Steps to Achieve Your Goals

_____

_____

_____

_____

_____

Reward

_____

THANKS, MOM

-Jenny

This month we celebrate Mother's Day, and I'd like to say thanks to my mom. I can't completely credit her for my desire to be a writer—I'm pretty sure I would have had that in me, regardless. But I can, and do, give her a tremendous amount of credit for never stomping on my dream. As an elementary and junior high school teacher, my mom encouraged hundreds of kids to read, write, and think creatively. But nobody benefited from it more than her two daughters.

A true lover of story, my mother slogged her way through my early manuscripts—the unpublishable messes I now refer to as "learning experiences"— without complaint. Abidingly positive, she can always find something good to say about what I've written. Even if I don't necessarily agree with her more critical assessments, they never fail to give me food for thought. Most importantly, she continues to stick with me through all my growing pains as a writer—which have lasted considerably longer than even the angst-filled teenage years.

I hope that when I'm my mother's age, I have her creative energy and enthusiasm for writing. I hope I can still dream big, as she does (though I will no doubt also share her inability to master any and all technological advances). And, boy, do I hope I've published a novel by then.

To my sons—thanks for making me a mom. I'll do my very best to support you in your creative endeavors—as long as they don't involve extreme tattoos or piercings, man-eating reptiles, speeds of greater than 75 miles per hour, clown college, changing your names to numbers, or throwing anything sharper than a Frisbee. And worms. You know how I feel about worms.

Finally, a few thoughts on mothers from some of the writers who have said it best:

And so our mothers and grandmothers have, more often than not anonymously, handed on the creative spark, the seed of the flower they themselves never hoped to see— or like a sealed letter they could not plainly read.

~Alice Walker

Thou art thy mother's glass, and she in thee Calls back the lovely April of her prime.

~William Shakespeare

My mother had a great deal of trouble with me, but I think she enjoyed it.

~Mark Twain

What women have inspired you in creativity and life?

WRITING AN EFFECTIVE QUERY LETTER FOR MAGAZINES

-Kerrie

A query is a one- to two-page sales pitch sent to an editor to see if she is interested in an article on the proposed topic. The query explains what will be in the article, shares why you are the perfect person to write it, and gives her a sample of your writing style. Editors are busy people, so they don't have time to read an inbox full of articles. The query letter helps streamline the process and gives the editor an opportunity to suggest a different angle or word count before you begin writing.

A query also saves you, the writer, some time. You can do initial research, make connections, and flesh out your idea. Once the assignment is made, you can then put in the needed time to write a fabulous article.

The format of a query letter is pretty simple.

SALUTATION: Dear _____:
Be sure to find out the name of the correct editor. Don't just put Dear Editor.

PARAGRAPH 1: Your hook or lead.

Get the editor interested in your idea with an interesting opening about your article. Start with a fact, an anecdote, a compelling question, something to hook the editor to want to read more.

PARAGRAPH 2: Body.

Share the key points of your article. Include some pertinent facts here to show the editor you understand the topic. If there are specific people you plan to interview, include that here as well.

PARAGRAPH 3: Offering.

What are you offering, and how will it affect the readers? "I am proposing a 1,000-word article highlighting the health benefits of dark chocolate. This article will educate your readers and show them that dark chocolate can be a valuable component of a healthy diet."

PARAGRAPH 4: Your qualifications.

What makes you the perfect person to write this article? Do you have any published clips (copy of published articles)? Do you have personal experience with this topic? Does your degree make you an expert? Even if you don't have any clips, explain why you are the person to write this article.

CLOSING: A call to action.

"I look forward to hearing from you soon." "Would you like me to send you the article?"

SIGNATURE:

Sign your name.

*Make sure to include your contact information in the query.

Do your research and put the time into writing an outstanding query letter. It can mean the difference between an acceptance letter and a no thank you.

REDISTRIBUTION OF POWER
-Kerrie

Recently my daughter auditioned for a local teen acting troupe. Before the auditions began, the director talked with the students about what they could expect from the audition, when they would find out who made it, and other bits of general information. But she ended with something that resonated with me and relates 100 percent to writers. She explained that there were only a few openings in the troupe, so not everyone was going to make it. Then with heartfelt conviction, she told those teens, "Don't ever base your self-worth as an actor on one audition. Do not give that power over to any director. It hasn't been earned, and they don't deserve it."

When I left, I couldn't stop thinking about what she said. So many times as writers we wrap up our self-worth in every query letter or proposal we send out. Then we wait for the response and rather than look at it as just that, a response, we use it to gauge our worth and abilities as a writer. If an editor/agent says yes, then we must be a good writer. If we get a no, then we must not be any good.

That *is* too much power to hand over to editors/agents and frankly, I don't think they want it. The agents and editors are only doing their job to make the best magazine, book, or anthology possible. It is up to us to be confident in our own abilities as a writer.

We have all heard those rejection letter examples from the likes of Stephen King, J. K. Rowling, and Dr. Seuss saying their writing wasn't any good. But what made these writers successful is that they didn't let an editor's opinion stop them. They were confident in their writing and they kept going. We all need to do the same.

Surround yourself with other positive writers, take classes, go to conferences, join a good critique group, and improve your craft so when you do send out your writing, you can rest assured that you sent out your best work, regardless of the response.

What do you think? Do we hand over our self-worth as writers to too many other people?

YOUR WRITING VOICE
-*Kerrie*

We all have unique qualities, inflections, tones in our speaking voice that help people identify who we are, even if they can't see us. The same thing happens in your writing. When writers find their voice, it becomes obvious to anyone reading their work. Think about it. Can you tell the difference between Stephen King, Tina Fey, and Jane Austen?

The problem is, many writers spend a lot of time trying to write like someone else. They want to be just like their favorite author. They end up copying their style and tone and in the end sound like an impersonator. They do not have their own identity.

The biggest factor in finding your writing voice is trust. You must trust yourself and your writing enough to get your thoughts and ideas on paper the way you want to write them. I know it can be difficult when you read an author who writes beautiful, flowing descriptions or one whose humor makes you laugh out loud. It can make you wish you could write like them. There is nothing wrong with learning from other writers and incorporating some of what they do into your writing, but don't go to such an extreme that it stifles your voice.

Finding your voice is not always an easy task, but it is a fun journey. You must write a lot and try out different styles and techniques. This is a time to try on those beautiful, flowing descriptions and that humor to see how it fits. Walk around in it a while, see how it feels. Use the parts that work for you—the parts that enhance your voice.

Eventually you will find your voice amongst it all. It will start shining through and be the one you want to spend the most time with, the one that you are at ease around. Your true voice is the one that flows naturally and from the core of who you are. It is the voice that made you fall in love with writing, the one that wants to be nurtured and tended to. It is this voice that wants to be heard.

What can you do to make sure you are honoring your own voice in your writing?

OH, SNAG!

-*Jenny*

In the grand scheme of things, my boys would probably rank clothes shopping somewhere between standardized testing and low-budget clowns. But they must occasionally accompany me to choose some new duds or risk dressing like castaways. The last time we were out, we discovered some lightweight athletic shirts we could all agree on. The boys loved the comfort and the colors, and I loved the price. The only problem—which we discovered when my younger son had a close encounter with Velcro and came away looking like a scratching post—is that they snag. On everything. I'm pretty sure I even saw a snag spontaneously burst forth, as if releasing some kind of freaky alien spores.

From gum in the dryer to interminable rush-hour detours, life is full of snags. So is writing. A writing snag is something that pulls a reader's mind in a distracting direction. A snag can come in any size—large (an entire scene that doesn't work), medium (an exchange of stilted dialogue), or small (a single wrongly placed letter). At a recent funeral, for example, I read in the program that the "internment" would immediately follow the service.

My brain: "Oh, snag."

Me: "What?"

Brain: "There's an extra 'n' in there. The proper word is 'interment.'"

Me: "You're really going to bring this up now? At a funeral?"

Brain: "Well, yes."

Me: "Ugh. We'll discuss it later."

As it turned out, that very afternoon I read a short story that mentioned the interment of a body.

My brain: "I told you so!"

Me: "Okay, okay. You don't need to gloat."

Internment means detention or imprisonment. *Interment* means burial or entombment. I suppose one could argue that a body is detained and/or imprisoned upon burial, but the words aren't truly synonymous. Hence the snag.

Keep a sharp eye out for snags, because a snag is how a Work In Progress (WIP) says, "Whoa, Bessie. There's trouble in these parts." (I'm not sure why I think a WIP would sound like an old-timey sheriff, but there you go.) So the next time you run across a snag, in your own writing or someone else's, stop and consider how to smooth it away. Because snags draw attention to our writing for all the wrong reasons . . . and they never fix themselves.

Have you encountered a writing snag?
How did/would you fix it?

JUNE

"You must keep sending work out; you must never let a manuscript do nothing but eat its head off in a drawer. You send that work out again and again, while you're working on another one. If you have talent, you will receive some measure of success— but only if you persist."
—Isaac Asimov

Writing Goals for the Month

_____

_____

_____

_____

Action Steps to Achieve Your Goals

_____

_____

_____

_____

Reward

_____

ORGANIZING YOUR QUERIES AND SUBMISSIONS

-Kerrie

When I started freelancing over a decade ago, it was clear early on that I would need to find a way to track my query submissions. My first plan of attack was a basic red spiral notebook. I would enter the date, the name of the query, and whom I sent it to. This worked okay, but I couldn't sort anything, and I was afraid of losing the notebook.

I then came up with the system I still use today. I have an Excel spreadsheet that I keep for anything I send out (queries, articles, proposals). To ensure the safekeeping of this document even more, I can put it on Google Drive so it is saved on "the cloud."

With Excel I can sort my information by date, title, publication. It really makes it easy when I want to see what I have sent to a certain publication or where I have sent a particular query.

Here are the headings I use for the columns:

Sent Out: The title of what I sent out
Type: Query, article, proposal

Publication/Agency: Where I sent it

Sent To: Specific person I sent it to

Email or address: The email address or snail mail address I sent it to

Date: Date I sent it

Response: The response from the editor: yes, no, maybe

Follow up: The date I followed up on what I sent

Notes: Miscellaneous notes, i.e., "Comment from editor said I was on the right track—send more"

My simple spreadsheet has helped me stay somewhat sane with tracking my submissions and has prevented me from sending duplicates to publications and editors.

Visit the Hot Chocolate Press website to download the spreadsheet.

http://hotchocolatepress.com

SUMMER HATS
-Jenny

I wear hats more often during the summer. In the literal sense, I have hats for watching baseball, hats for gardening, hats for hanging out at the pool, and hats that I hope just look cute while keeping the sun off my freckles. I wear many figurative summer hats as well, including those of chauffeur, chef/short order cook, referee, recreation director, park ranger, personal shopper, tour guide, nurse, arbitrator, dog walker, party planner, and banker.

And writer. I shouldn't forget that one.

Actually, it's easy to forget to put on my writer hat during the summer, partly because of general busy-ness and partly because I usually catch a pretty good case of the lazy, school's out vibe from my boys. This lack of scheduled writing time used to make me panic, and I would resign myself to eleven or so totally unproductive weeks.

But a couple of years ago, I noticed something: my writer brain does not take the summers off. It is always there, always observing, always piecing together random phrases and bits of dialogue. In fact, it is often busiest when I am not sitting down and telling it to write. It works in the quiet mornings before my boys wake up. It works as I'm pulling weeds, watering flowers, and waging my annual war on squash bugs. It works in the soft evening light as I'm waiting for a baseball game to start.

My writer brain also works when I am reading. I'm no different from most in that I like to have fun, exciting, engaging books on my summer reading list—good beach reads, or, more likely in my case, good wish-I-was-at-the-beach reads. My writer brain reads them over my shoulder, telling me, "oh, I like that," or "no, I would have done that differently."

In the generally unstructured days of summer, my writer brain and I find a balance. I try to give it fertile moments, and it gives me food for thought. I sneak away for some computer time, and it does not let me spend that time looking at Awkward Family Photos. And then, when school is back in session and I can start removing hats à la Dr. Seuss's Bartholomew Cubbins, I find that my writer hat has been waiting patiently for me all along. And with any luck, it still fits.

Are you able to keep your writer hat on during the summer?

18 Verbs to Avoid

-Kerrie

Analyze a sample of your writing. What happens when you rewrite a passage and replace the following verbs with different ones? Does your writing seem stronger now? I bet it does. I challenge you for the next month to not use any of these verbs in your writing. Use stronger verbs instead and see how it impacts your writing.

18 Verbs to Avoid

appear	feel	seen
are	had	smell
become	has	taste
did	have	turn
do	is	was
done	look	were

RUNNING THE RACE

-Kerrie

"I am here for a purpose and that purpose is to grow into a mountain, not to shrink to a grain of sand. Henceforth will I apply ALL my efforts to become the highest mountain of all and I will strain my potential until it cries for mercy."

~Og Mandino

We all have a passion for writing. It is something we are drawn to, something we feel we have to do. It is our purpose in life to share our thoughts, feelings, ideas, and stories with the world. Once we recognize that writing is our purpose, our calling, then we have a responsibility to fulfill it. We must grow into that mountain that Og Mandino was talking about.

One of our biggest hurdles is not staying connected to our passion and the joy associated with writing. We allow negative thoughts to fill our mind, instantly stopping our creativity. We receive a response from an editor or agent saying they are not interested in our work and it all starts. "I am not a good writer." "Who was I kidding anyway?" "Why am I putting myself through this?" "I will never get published."

Like the quote says, "I am here for a purpose and that purpose is to grow into a mountain, not to shrink to a grain of sand." It is those challenging times that call us to remember our purpose. It is during these times that we must not shrink and become a grain of sand.

One of my favorite passages from the Bible is from Hebrews 12:1. It says, "Let us run with endurance, the race God has set before us." Regardless of your spiritual beliefs or religious affiliations, the meaning behind this quote is the same. We all have a specific race we are running, and we must endure through the good and bad times. There will be detours and hills along the way, but we can take comfort in knowing we are running the race we were meant to run and victory awaits us.

What are you doing to stay in the race?

CAPTURING THE ELUSIVE

-Jenny

I have a hummingbird feeder hanging outside my front window. Every summer, I typically have one or two regular customers. This year, though, no such luck. I heard the birds buzzing to and fro around the neighborhood, so I knew they had returned. But why were they giving me the brush off?

I wondered if a different feeder would help. The old one was impossible to clean, anyway. So I bought a new one, filled it with fresh, homemade nectar, and hung it in the same spot. The next morning, I thoughtlessly threw back the curtain, and, lo and behold, there was the hummingbird. For one split-second, he hung above the feeder, shimmering like an ornament. Then he zoomed off. As far as I can tell, the little sucker hasn't been back. (But I have no shortage of sugar-loving wasps.)

I'm pretty sure my abrupt opening of the curtain scared the bird away for good. Hummingbird season in my part of town is short, and I'm disappointed that I'll have to wait another year to try again. But it got me thinking about how creative-types try to capture the elusive. Wildlife photographers sit in blinds for hours waiting for the blink-and-you-miss-it shot. Actors rehearse, balancing craft and chemistry until their performances become much more than merely "playing a part."

Writers capture the elusive, too, in a variety of forms—an astoundingly unique plot twist, for example. Spot-on dialogue. A succinctly evocative descriptive passage. On the rare occasion, when I sit down to write, the elusive is not so elusive. My characters go above and beyond, surprising me with their inventiveness. The completed pages pile up. I am, as the athletes say, in the zone.

Other times, it all flies out the window. Every paragraph is work. My characters are dull and two-dimensional. Their dialogue stinks. They couldn't care less about making my life easy, and the more I nag them, the more they resist. The farther I toss out that net, the wider they disperse.

So, what's the cure, what coaxes the elusive near enough to hold? Patience . . . give it time. Perseverance . . . don't give up. Progress . . . keep the forward momentum going, even if it means switching to another project. Preparation . . . set an inviting table, and see who shows up.

How do you capture the elusive in your writing?

JULY

"The difference between the right word and the almost right word is the difference between lightning and a lightning bug."
—*Mark Twain*

Writing Goals for the Month

_____

_____

_____

_____

_____

Action Steps to Achieve Your Goals

_____

_____

_____

_____

_____

Reward

_____

DECLARING INDEPENDENCE
-Jenny

Happy Independence Day, everyone! Though July 4th marks the celebration of an American holiday, independence, as we've seen in such dramatic examples from around the world, is an idea that has no geographic or political boundaries. Independence inspires revolution and builds nations, but it works on a smaller scale, too. Fledglings seek independence from the nest. Kids seek independence from their parents. Cats seek independence from everyone.

In the spirit of the day, let's all take a moment to declare independence from something that's holding us back in our writing lives. Perhaps you belong to a critique group that doesn't meet your needs, but you're reluctant to call it quits because they're such nice people—and the snacks are delicious. Or maybe you need to put a little distance between yourself and social media. It's fun, and it can be useful, but it can also be a huge distraction. Maybe I'm wrong, but I'm willing to bet that whatever your long-lost friend from third grade is doing these days, it's not as important as your WIP. (If you went to school with Michelle Obama, I take that back.)

Today, I'm declaring independence from the word "never." I have nothing against the word itself—it's a fine word that can have great dramatic effect. One of my favorite examples comes from the movie *Batman Begins*. The stately Wayne Manor, besieged by a gang of vigilantes, is burning. Bruce Wayne is trapped. After loyal butler Alfred (whose last name, by the way, is Pennyworth) dodges flaming debris to rescue his billionaire boss, Bruce asks, "You still haven't given up on me?" And Alfred replies, "Never." Because Alfred is played by Michael Caine, it sounds like "*Nev*-ah." Which makes it even better.

But many writers use "never" in self-defeating ways. We say we'll *never* finish our novels, *never* get published, *never* make any money, *never* get our big break. Used thusly, "never" becomes a heavy anchor around the neck, and who has the desire or strength to carry that around all day? So I'm going to try and use "never" only in contexts that I'm certain are true (I'll never be 5'7" tall) or affirming (never give up).

Take notice, all you negative *nevers*. I'm kicking you to the curb.

As for my old nemesis, chocolate, well, that truly is a case of never say never.

From what will you declare your independence today?

CAN HEADLINES HELP US?

-Kerrie

Today's headlines rang out with sadness. Plane Crash Kills 50, Children Killed in Afghan Fight, and Female Bomber Kills 39. My heart goes out to all the families affected by these tragedies and deaths.

As a writer, I am always fascinated by human behavior. I constantly wonder what is going on in the mind of a person such as the female suicide bomber. What made her so committed and passionate about her cause that she was willing to take her own life and the lives of those around her? What was she thinking about before she committed this horrific act against humanity? What did she do that morning? Did she have a family? Did she cook them breakfast like it was a normal day? Was she an angry person?

These types of events make me realize that many times, fact can be far stranger and more awful than fiction. But, as writers, we can draw upon these events. We can imagine digging deep into the psyche of real-life heroes and martyrs and begin to form believable characters and intriguing story lines.

Using this headline, you could create a story about a young Iraqi girl who grew up constantly seeking her father's approval, becoming passionate about his causes, and doing all she could to show him that she was worthy of his love. This would lead to her final attempt and ultimately, her death.

Are there any of today's headlines that you could incorporate into your novel or use as the basis of a short story or essay?

STUCK IN THE MIDDLE
-*Jenny*

To all gardeners who are enjoying the fruits—and veggies—of your labors, my sun hat is off to you. My garden is pretty sad. Although I've gotten a couple of decent zucchinis and a few cherry tomatoes, the rest looks . . . unmotivated. The usually reliable beans, peas, and broccoli have done zip-nothin'. Same for the yellow squash. The herbs are wilting in the heat, though I am able to rouse them to semiconsciousness with daily watering.

The other day, I was tempted to pull most of it out and replace it with something foolproof. Plastic daisies from the craft store, maybe. Tacky, sure, but sturdy enough to survive a Colorado hailstorm. But when I looked at the calendar, I realized that it's only the middle of summer. With any luck, I still have at least two good months of growing season, and a lot can happen in two months. (Yeah, I'm looking at you, broccoli.)

The middle can be a sticky place. The excitement of beginning is a memory, and the finished product is barely visible over the hill. Things in the middle may not look as you expected. They may be better, or they may be worse. They may require much more work than you ever anticipated. But they may also be hinting at rewards you never dreamed of. They may point you in an entirely new direction.

I am referring to gardens. But I'm also referring to any project that takes weeks/months/years to complete, such as—oh, gosh, let me see—a manuscript. If you're feeling stuck in the middle of one of those, I wish I could offer you some easy solutions, such as Miracle-Gro or hungry ladybugs. Lacking that, my best advice is to keep at it. Put in the daily work. Tend what you've done and encourage new growth. Spend a quiet moment appreciating what you've accomplished. Don't focus on the weeds, for those can be pulled out later. Celebrate each success, no matter how small. My first cherry tomato of the season was tiny, but it packed a lot of flavor.

What do you do when you're feeling stuck in the middle with your writing?

You Know You Are a Writer When . . .

-Kerrie & Jenny

It is impossible for you to read a book without a red pen in hand, so you can edit the *already published and edited* book.

You go to set the table and you find ideas you had jotted down on a napkin—a cloth napkin.

You dread facing the blank computer screen so much that you you'd rather pick the grime out of your stove with a toothpick than sit down and start writing.

You find yourself saying, "Gee, Beth, I'm sorry your dog died . . . but can I write a story about it?"

You move your bed into the dining room and your computer into your bedroom so you can claim your bedroom as a home office on your taxes.

You become so engrossed in your writing that you

constantly embarrass your children because you're still in your pajamas when you pick them up from school.

Your fictional characters become so real that you start adding them to your prayer list.

You walk into your bedroom at night and your spouse has set the mood—candles, music—for a romantic evening. You say, "Not tonight, honey, I've got to keep writing."

You do your best thinking in the shower. When your family asks why there's no hot water, you tell them the pilot light went out . . . again.

You've left the house wearing shoes, socks, and earrings that don't match. At the same time.

The only Academy Award that makes you cry is the one for Best Original Screenplay.

You still buy food in alphabet shapes even though your kids are in college.

SUNSHINE SHOULDN'T STOP US

-Kerrie

I should move to Seattle! I love to write when it is raining outside. A freshly steeped cup of jasmine tea next to me, a candle burning brightly, and the pitter patter of the rain on the windows and roof stir up my creative muse. My words flow and time becomes irrelevant.

Well, the issue for me is I don't live in Seattle, I live in Colorado where we average 300 days of sunshine a year. The blue sky, fresh air, and mountains frequently try to lure me away from the computer to come out and play.

At our Northern Colorado Writers coffee yesterday this very issue came up. How do you stay motivated to write during the summer? Some ideas were thrown around, such as take your writing outside, spend more time reading, allow yourself extra time to be outdoors.

Then someone said it shouldn't matter. It shouldn't matter what the weather is like or what time of year it is. If you are committed to your writing then you will stick with your routine and write. You will make the time to crank out those words and prioritize your writing.

It was hard to argue with that logic, and no one did. The truth is, this is the advice given by many famous authors like Stephen King, John Grisham, and Janet Evanovich: if you want to be a writer then you need to write every day.

So maybe what we need to do as writers is take the inscription that hangs in a New York City post office, "Neither snow nor rain nor heat nor gloom of night stays these couriers from the swift completion of their appointed rounds," adapt it for us, and hang it by our workspace: "Neither snow nor rain nor heat nor gloom of night stays these writers from the swift completion of their work in progress."

How much time do you devote to your writing
and how do you stay committed to that time?

AUGUST

"If we did all the things we are capable of doing, we
would literally astound ourselves."
—*Thomas Edison*

Writing Goals for the Month

_____

_____

_____

_____

_____

Action Steps to Achieve Your Goals

_____

_____

_____

_____

_____

Reward

_____

IN THE BEGINNING . . . IN MEDIA RES

-Kerrie

Where to begin or not to begin—that is the question. Many writers (including me) tend to fall short when it comes to the beginning of our writing, whether it is a novel, short story, or magazine article. We want to give all the background, set up the scene, and gently introduce the reader to our character or topic. It seems to make sense when we are writing because we forget that we have all the other information in our head. We know how the murder happens and gets solved, we know how the hero and heroine get together at the end. We know it all. The reader enters our world—fiction or nonfiction—completely in the dark.

In media res is a Latin phrase that means "in the middle of things" and is an effective way to start our writing. You drop your readers into the middle of a scene, already in progress. The idea is to hook them and compel them to keep reading.

Here is an example from Melina Bellows's novel, *Wish*:

> Is he dead? I jump off my Vespa and race past a fire engine, an ambulance, and the F.D.N.Y. scrimmage blocking my street. There, in front of my apartment, is my brother's body, sprawled on the sidewalk.

We are immediately put into the middle of a scene. Bellows didn't take three pages to introduce us to her main character. She got us hooked right away. She has the rest of the book to tell us about the character and the story. But now, as the reader, you want to know what happened and if the brother is really dead.

You can do same thing in nonfiction. Here is an example from an article I found on NPR, from the Associated Press:

> First, there was a run on energy-efficient light bulbs. When those ran out, people began asking for lamp oil. But when they started demanding clothespins in this land of mist and rain, it was clear Alaska's capital city was caught in a serious energy crunch.

This scene is not as action-packed as the first example, but it does the same thing. It shows us what is going on right now. It paints a scene. Then it goes back to explain how Juneau got to this point.

Give this technique a try with your own work and see what happens. You will find your writing will pack a punch right out of the gate. Then it is your job to keep your readers hanging on.

THE "A" CIRCLE

-Jenny

I know *The "A" Circle* sounds like a place where Brangelina Pitt-Jolie might hang out, so let me clarify. I recently heard literary agent Sara Megibow talk about the things authors must do before they can even think about getting published.

Sara began by stretching out her arms, making a circle, and saying (I'll paraphrase) here you writers are, in your circles, being artists. Then she stepped to the side and made another circle to describe her space, the publishing biz. I'll call that *The "B" Circle.* A for Artist, B for Business—you're with me here, right?

The majority of Sara's class addressed the ways in which writers can increase their chances of gaining access to that coveted "B" Circle of agent representation and, hopefully, publication. Good news: it doesn't involve sacrificing live chickens! Unless your book happens to be about sacrificing chickens. Or you've written a short story collection, in which case you might also need to hire a voodoo priestess, as agents typically don't clamber for those.

For the rest of the evening, I found myself mentally returning to the image of the artist's circle. I think of myself as a number of things: mother, wife, sister, daughter, competent wordsmith (on a good day), hopeless wanna-be (on a bad one), friend of Gayle and Dr. Phil (oh, wait, that's Oprah). But I never think of myself as an artist, so having an industry professional call me that, albeit indirectly, made me feel kinda warm and fuzzy inside.

But then I tried to picture my circle, where I presumably work and am happily artistic and drink wine—or at least learn how to spell gewürztraminer. The image that came to mind was less like a circle and more like . . . an amoeba. Sort of shapeless, with a highly permeable outer membrane that lets in all sorts of distractions—phone calls, Cakewrecks, jalapeno-cheddar potato chips, nagging self-doubt.

Oh, my. Time to shape up my circle.

Lacking an actual human-sized hamster ball in which I can curl up and be an artist while gnawing on seeds and dried corn, my circle will have to be a virtual one. I imagine it as a shining bubble around me that is ionized to let in the positive writer juju and deflect the negative. And with every keystroke—even the backspaces; those are important, too—it grows brighter and stronger, bathing me in creativity while giving me an awesome sunless tan.

Much better.

Do you think of yourself as an artist? Do you have a space to call your circle?

DON'TS OF QUERYING
AN AGENT
-Kerrie

This past Saturday, at a Northern Colorado Writers workshop, Kate Schafer Testerman, with KT Literary out of Denver, shared with the attendees some tips of what *not* to do when querying an agent. These are all things she has seen authors do at one time or another.

DON'T have a spokesperson write the query. Write it yourself. It doesn't make you look good to have your best friend or mother send the query because you are too shy or you don't want your feelings hurt.

DON'T have your main character write the query — the letter should be in your voice.

DON'T imagine accolades, meaning don't say that your book is sure to win a Pulitzer Prize or Newberry Award.

DON'T use other people (not in the publishing industry) as references. "My third-grade class thought this was the best book they ever read." "My mother loved it!"

DON'T preach. If there is a lesson in the book, you should not have to explain it.

DON'T design the book. There is no need to include what illustrations you envision for a picture book, what you want the cover to look like, how you want the pages laid out . . . this is just a query. You have to sell the idea first.

DON'T ignore the agent's submission guidelines— they are there for a reason. You need to show enough respect for that agent to follow what they have asked.

DON'T send a generic form letter that clearly is being sent to a bunch of agents. Personalize each letter you send out. Although the content of most of your letter is probably the same to the different agents you are sending it to, there are ways you can customize it for each one.

DON'T list unrelated accomplishments. For example, if you are writing a romance, the fact that you have a degree in chemical engineering or love to scuba dive is totally irrelevant.

DON'T forget to put your name and email on your query.

DON'T forget to proofread.

By keeping these DON'Ts in mind, you will find more success in your quest to find and agent.

BE A GOOD SPORT

-*Jenny*

My older son's baseball team didn't win a game this season. They lost some close ones, some blowouts, and some games they should have won. It was a frustrating experience, but the boys showed amazing character. They went out and played hard every time. They didn't quit. And they didn't turn on each other. Even more impressively, neither did the parents or coaches. It's impressive because adults often seem to feel entitled to indulge in poor sportsmanship. Judging from industry blogs, writers are no exception.

So, a quiz: Aspiring Author is looking for agency representation. She does her research and finds the perfect Agent, a match surely made in publishing heaven. She crafts a personalized query letter and sends it per submission guidelines. Then—in a day, a week, a month—the unthinkable happens. She receives a "no, thanks" from Agent. Aspiring Author is floored. Obviously, Agent wouldn't recognize a best-seller if it was hand-delivered by Hemingway's ghost. Aspiring Author (who now suffers from major Hurt Feelings) should

a) Immediately call the agency, ask to speak to Agent, and, when the request is denied, berate the receptionist until s/he hangs up;

b) Take her case to Twitter. "Agnt sux bcuz . . ."

c) Write a blog post titled "Top 10 Reasons Agent Is Not Qualified to Carry My Book Bag;"

d) Create a claymation video depicting Agent being flattened under her slush pile. Post it on YouTube;

e) Reject the rejection in a reply email. Throw in some mild profanity. Ignore spelling and grammar—agents don't care about that stuff, anyway;

f) Resubmit from a different email address every day for as long as humanly possible; or

g) Be a good sport. Understand that virtually every writer gets turned down many, many times. Vent in private. Cry a little. Eat too much chocolate. Then get back on the horse and start querying elsewhere.

The answer, of course, is "g." (I know none of you would even consider doing otherwise. But everyone knows someone who knows someone.) Yes, there are bad agents out there, and any unethical behavior should be exposed ASAP. But, remember— the best way for a writer to trash his/her reputation is to publicly trash someone else's.

Rising Up Above the Masses

−Kerrie

I stare at my underwater screen saver. Colorful fish swim around, just like the thoughts in my brain. I keep tilting my head, hoping the stuff in there will either fall out or magically organize itself so I can think clearly again. It's no use though; the only thing I seem to be accomplishing is a stiff neck.

One month ago, life seemed good. I sent out query after query, and as I pressed send for each email, I knew no editor could refuse my brilliant ideas. After all, I had done my homework by feverishly perusing the *Writer's Market*, I had attended writers conferences, I had been published in *Better Homes and Gardens* (only once, but it was a great moment). I was no amateur writer!

Now I feel as if my life is on a downward spiral. I talk to myself each time I open my email.

"Today is the day! I am going to find a contract in my inbox and an assignment for three more stories." Then I start playing games in my head.

"Get real. There won't be anything except more rejections."

"No, today will be different!!"

"Oh please, get a grip."

"No, really. I . . . I know it will be different today."

"Yeah, right!"

I pause before opening my email. I seem to be moving in slow motion as I click on my mailbox. I close my eyes quickly, then slowly open one. There in the middle of my inbox is a response from an editor. With a trembling hand I click on it thinking maybe this is the one!

"Dear Writer (this is never a good sign), Thank you for submitting your article idea BUT . . ."

With a big sigh I close down my email. Why do I keep doing this to myself? Why don't I just give up?

All writers at one time or another have hit a moment like this, one where nothing seems to be going right. We feel like we must be horrible writers because no one seems to want our articles, books, short stories, plays. Nothing is selling.

It is in these moments that true writers emerge and (using the well-known cliché) the women are separated from the girls and the men from the boys. The die-hard writers are the ones that push through these moments when others fall away. They are the ones that sit back down at their computer and start writing again. They are the ones that get published.

So, what kind of writer are you going to be?

Are you going to dwell among the masses who gave up and never reached their full potential or are you going to rise above that and keep writing—even when it feels impossible?

SEPTEMBER

"This is how you do it: you sit down at the keyboard
and you put one word after another until it's done.
It's that easy, and that hard."
—Neil Gaiman

Writing Goals for the Month

_____

_____

_____

_____

_____

Action Steps to Achieve Your Goals

_____

_____

_____

_____

_____

Reward

_____

MEET MY NEW BOSS

-Jenny

I recently had the rare opportunity to observe my husband in work mode when a department remodel meant a week of telecommuting for him. In general, he doesn't like to work from home, but the prospect of dodging electricians and carpet-layers convinced him.

On the first day, I was curious how things would play out, so I spied on him. He had the occasional snack, he took a short break for lunch, but otherwise, he sat at his desk and worked. (Exciting, right? Well, it's IT, not the bomb squad.) When his day ended, he turned off his computer. The next morning, he got up and did it all again.

I used to be like that when I worked at a "real" job. I had an *In* basket and an *Out* basket, and I moved things from *In* to *Out* as efficiently as possible. I knew what I had to do and how long I had to do it. My lunch break was half an hour, and any conversations with coworkers about non-work topics lasted only a few minutes.

Jeez, what happened to me?

The likeliest explanation is that I quit my job to stay home with my kids. (Which, by the way, is a decision I will never, ever regret.) Anyone who has been home with a child or two knows that scheduled blocks of time longer than five minutes can be hard to come by, especially in the years between two-naps-a-day and elementary school. Even though my boys are well into their school careers—but thankfully still too young for driving and mustaches—this mind-set persists. My years of mom-training mean that after spending between thirty seconds and fifteen minutes at my computer, I quite often have a sudden and uncontrollable urge to jump up and do something else. And so I do. The "something else" varies—it might be laundry, spontaneous toilet repair, or eating enough chocolate chips to kill a mongoose—but it is definitely *not* writing.

Thanks to my husband's week of working from home, I've been inspired to try a new plan: when I sit down to write, I'm going to pretend that I'm telecommuting and that someone, somewhere, is monitoring my productivity. I can't think of a better person for the job than George Jetson's boss, the irascible Mr. Spacely. Sure, he's a cartoon, but he has a big voice for a little guy, and I don't want him yelling at me every time I get up out of my chair. If he works out, my next step is getting Rosie the Robot to clean my house.

How do you keep yourself on task when working at home?

FINDING YOUR
CREATIVE SPACE

-Kerrie

Over the past month, a few amazing things have happened that have impacted my writing life and allowed me to find my creative space again.

In the latter part of the summer until early fall, I found it difficult to do any writing that wasn't related to Northern Colorado Writers. People would ask what I was writing and I would say, "website content and emails." No, they would say, *your* writing. I'd pause and confess, "Nothing. I haven't written anything of my own."

As the director of a writing organization, this is a hard thing to admit. Here I am offering suggestions to other writers about their writing and how to organize their lives to fit it in, and I can't even do it myself.

My problem was all in my head—literally. Thoughts of work, ideas, family issues, finances, all whirled around in my head like a tornado spinning out of control, and I couldn't figure out how to stop it.

At the end of the summer, I took two weeks off from work hoping that would help, but all that did was move the location of all the stress. I still had access to my computer, I still read emails everyday, and the F4 twister in my head showed no signs of downgrading to anywhere near an F1.

So, when my friend, also one of my daughter's high school teachers, asked if I would help chaperone a week-long school fly-fishing adventure trip with 21 high school students, I was hesitant. First of all, I didn't know how to fly fish, and second, how could I possibly leave with all that I felt I had going on?

With some coaxing and my insistence on being in charge of the food and cooking, he convinced me to go.

Being away from my computer, phone, and anything else feeding the tornado caused it to lose its momentum. Add the fresh air, hours by the river, and beautiful scenery, and clarity soon followed. I was soon able to "see" just how cluttered my creative space had become.

It was no wonder I couldn't do any writing. I started reorganizing everything in my head and was able to clear out a small space to do a little journaling (it's all about baby steps).

Upon our return home, the twister started again. With less "junk" swirling around, it wasn't quite as strong as before, but it was still there, intruding on my creative space. The good news is, I had found enough clarity to see what I needed to do.

With the encouragement of some friends, I decreased the NCW studio hours by two hours a day and made a plan to take one day a week off in order to open up some time for me to write. I also needed to schedule times away from my computer (ideally outside). This is where the fly fishing comes back in.

The first time I actually got to fish, I fell in love with it. I can absolutely see this being my new favorite downtime activity away from my computer. At the end of that day fishing, my mind was effectively cleared, allowing even more creative space to open up.

Because of all that, I have been able to start writing again. The last two mornings I got up around 5:45 a.m. to write in my journal. Both days I was able to crank out eight pages, and it felt great. Tomorrow I plan to do the same thing.

Then to top it all off, I am going fishing!

What is the condition of your internal creative space?

THE VOICES IN MY HEAD
-Jenny

My boys have been in school for three weeks now, and the soundtrack that accompanies summer vacation at my house has come to an end. During the day, I no longer hear brothers joking around, telling stories, and picking on each other. I'm not serenaded by trumpet and guitar practice or Harry Potter and Star Wars video games. No teenagers drop by with their boisterous voices and carefree door-slamming.

Until about 3:00 in the afternoon, it's pretty darn quiet around here. I hear the occasional lawn mower, my washing machine thumps and spins, my old dog thwacks her tail when she thinks something food-related might happen. But this September silence is not such a bad thing, because it helps me hear the voices in my head.

Lest you worry about my health, mental and otherwise, rest assured that I'm not having auditory hallucinations. Also known as *paracusia*, they can be indicative of schizophrenia, temporal lobe epilepsy, brain tumors, Wilson's disease, porphyria, sarcoidosis, and a bunch of other stuff I've happily never heard of.

No, my condition is more along the lines of Chronic Mental Composing of Conversations Between New and/or Familiar Imagined Characters Who Just Might Want Me to Write (or Keep Writing) About Them Someday in the Immediate or Distant Future. Because that's pretty lengthy—even by medical standards—it's easier to say that my affliction is known as Being a Writer.

I'm certainly glad to have ears that work, for I enjoy listening to music and NPR and snarky coffee-shop patrons. But silence helps me by making room in my head for some good old creative cognition. Someone famous probably already said this, but a writer who is alone with his or her thoughts is never really alone. We can, and do, fit entire worlds in our heads. What's more, we give the characters who live there something to talk about.

So what are the voices in my head saying these days? Some are introducing themselves for the first time, some are complaining that I've been ignoring them (they've got me there, I'm afraid), and others are informing me that they took a vote while I was at the pool and they want a comprehensive plot revision and better dental. And they're all reminding me that summer is over, and it's time to get busy.

What are your writing voices telling you?

YOUR WRITING KNAPSACK
-Kerrie

Writing is definitely a long journey with many adventures along the way. When I began this trek, my writing knapsack was light. I had a journal, a pen, and lots of ideas. I set off, excited to get to that magical land called Publishing where I was sure all my writing dreams would come true.

But not long into the journey it became quite clear that I needed more supplies. I grabbed a *Writer's Market* and added it to my knapsack. I realized there were many roads to publication: agents, editors, magazines, literary journals, contests, and more. I liked the look of the magazine path and headed off in that direction.

On this path, I found resources on writing for magazines, like Jenna Glatzer's book, *Make a Real Living as a Freelance Writer*, and *Writer's Digest Magazine*. I soon found other writers on the trail. Some had been there a while. Others were new like me. One led me on a shortcut where I found and hooked up with a critique group. Once back on the trail, I stopped at writers conferences and continued talking to those I met along the way.

Even with my limited amount of tools I did end up in the land called Publishing, but it was the outskirts. I realized this land was huge and was going to take more tools and a lot of time to explore. But I was excited about the possibilities and was ready to continue exploring.

Over the years I have added more resources, information, and contacts to my writing knapsack. It has become quite heavy, but everything in there has helped me and continues to help me on my writing journey.

Here are the top five things I have in my Writing Knapsack:

- *Writer's Market*
- Stephen King's memoir *On Writing*
- A list of contacts I have met along the way
- My laptop
- My Journal

What are your top five items in your Writing Knapsack?

1. _____
2. _____
3. _____
4. _____
5. _____

OCTOBER

"A good novel tells us the truth about its hero; but a
bad novel tells us the truth about its author."
—*Gilbert K. Chesterton*

Writing Goals for the Month

_____

_____

_____

_____

_____

Action Steps to Achieve Your Goals

_____

_____

_____

_____

_____

Reward

_____

FOURTH-QUARTER
GAME PLANS
-Jenny

I'll say this quietly so as not to unduly alarm anyone: it's October. I find it hard to believe, as it feels as though we were just celebrating the Fourth of July. But because my phone, my computer, and my desk and wall calendars are all in agreement, I must accept the fact that we are now entering the fourth quarter of the year.

In terms of personal productivity, that fact is daunting. But as any good sports fan knows, a lot can happen in the fourth quarter. Take the 1989 Lakers vs. Sonics Western Conference Semifinals game four. The Lakers were down by as many as 29 in the first half but came back to win 97–95—and sweep the series.

Or how about the New York Jets, who were trailing the Miami Dolphins 30–7 in the fourth quarter but won 40–37? (I wish I could claim to be awesome-sports-stat-gal, but I had to rely on Google for these.)

Writers, today is the perfect time to examine your fourth-quarter game plan. Perhaps you've had a great year so far. You've put a lot of points on the board, you're well ahead of the game, and you're ready to ease up a little and maybe head to the locker room early. I say, good for you, congratulations, job well done.

But maybe you're more like me—you've had your share of punts, fumbles, and miscues. You can't seem to get out of the hole, and you're starting to hear the rustling sound of fans leaving early. Well, it's not too late to shake things up.

That might mean digging in and working harder. Or it might mean working smarter by using what you learned in the first three quarters to put your biggest obstacles behind you. It might even take a gutsy call, such as committing to NaNoWriMo in November. My point is that there is enough time left to make solid progress toward your writing goals.

If you've put in too much time on the sidelines this year, join me in getting up off the bench. I'm tying my shoes right now. For further inspiration, I might put up a picture of Eli Manning, who in 2011 tied an NFL record with seven fourth-quarter comebacks and went on to win the Super Bowl. Not too shabby.

What's included in your writer's game plan
for the end of this year?

A Little Help from My Friends

-Kerrie

I would not be the writer I am today without my incredible critique group. For the past 15 years, I have been meeting with this group every Wednesday evening from 7:00 to 10:00 at Ellen's house. When I joined the group, it had already been around for about 20 years. Members have come and gone, but we have a strong core group that isn't going anywhere.

Most groups have a name like Raintree Writers or Broad Horizons, but we call ourselves Writers Group. We didn't really pick this name because we wanted it; it became assigned to us by default because we could never agree on a name. We needed something to say when a spouse or friends would ask, "where are you going?" Our reply was Writers Group.

Earlier this week at Writers Group, we decided to try something new and have a Submission Night. The goal was for everyone to come to group with up to three pieces of work they wanted to find potential markets for. We wanted to do this because we knew some members had great projects gathering dust and it was time for them to be sent out again.

We got to Ellen's house early, enjoyed a wonderful dinner together, and then got right to work. Each one of us had a piece of chart paper with our name on it where we listed our three books or articles needing a home. We briefly discussed everyone's projects and narrowed down genres, age groups, and core themes.

We then broke out all our market books (*Writer's Market, Best of Magazine Markets 2013, 2013 Novel and Short Story Writer's Market*) and started researching. The idea was, as we looked through the market guide for places to send our projects, we could also be looking for everyone else as well. When we found a potential market for someone, we wrote the publisher/agent/magazine name on a sticky note, with a quick note as to why we picked this market, and then put the sticky on that person's chart paper.

After about two and a half hours our eyes glazed over and we couldn't see straight anymore, so we stopped. Everyone's chart paper averaged about eight new potential markets. We ended the night by breaking out the champagne and imagining a year had passed. We raised our glasses and toasted our success in finding publishers, agents, and editors who wanted to publish our work.

This process strengthened our support for one another even more, it made researching markets fun, and it provided the incentive to start sending out submissions again.

I highly recommend trying this with your critique group or with a group of trusted writing friends.

THE RANDOM NAME GAME
-*Jenny*

Not being a soda drinker, I rarely order anything other than water in a restaurant. But occasionally, I will opt for half lemonade, half iced tea. You may know this drink as an Arnold Palmer. I refuse to call it that, because for some reason, the name is difficult for me to enunciate. I have to stop and think about it to make sure it comes out right, and even then I feel like I have a cherry pit rolling around on my tongue. And no offense to the famous golfer in question, but not even James Bond would sound cool ordering an Arnold Palmer, even if he followed it up with "shaken, not stirred." Or in my case, slurred.

Names in general can be vexing—remembering them, spelling them, pronouncing them, and giving them to our characters. If we all wrote like Dickens, we could get away with Canon Crisparkle and Polly Toodle. Dickens aside, some of literature's best character names—Jay Gatsby, Scarlett O'Hara, Atticus Finch, Clarissa Dalloway—are unique but not outrageous. And they're pronounceable. (Sorry, Holden Caulfield, you don't make my list. It's another cherry pit thing.)

The telephone book (remember those things?) used to be my go-to in the hunt for character names. It's amazing how many people out in the world have interesting monikers. Baby name lists identify trends, which may lead to names you want to use or want to avoid. If lists in general are too tedious, how about a random name generator? (For your characters, not your kids.) I played around with one the other day, and here are some of the suggestions it gave me.

Female: Laurie Deneau, Michelle Olivier, Lorhonda Mallon, Dora Lehman, April Schroeder

Male: Bill Katz, Hunter Nichols, Walker Powell, Metcalf Brown, Marshall Katz (Great, now I'm wondering which one of the Katz brothers is the evil twin.)

I kept at it for a while, as it was kind of addictive, and came up with a good dozen names I wouldn't turn down. The rest didn't make the cut, but even I have to admit that the random name generator beats the phone book any day. Whatever character name you choose, you might want to run it by friends or a critique group to make sure they can get their mouths around it.

Take a few minutes to play around with a name generator, and write down the names you lik

REACHING YOUR FULL POTENTIAL

-Kerrie

Raise your hand if you are a writer. Now, keep your hand up if you feel you are reaching your full potential as a writer. Many hands come down (including mine).

Even when we identify ourselves as writers, we are not doing all we can to be the best we can be. Distractions get in our way, and writing is no longer a priority. A constant cloud of guilt hangs over us because we know we should be devoting more time to this literary craft we love, yet we refuse to make room on our overflowing plate.

We can't possibly do and be everything all at once; choices have to be made. But as certain things are cut out of our lives, it opens up our plates and enables us to have more time to reach our full potential.

In order to do this you must examine your life closely and figure out what your priorities are. In LeAnn Thieman's book *Balancing Life in Your War*

Zones: A Guide to Physical, Mental, and Spiritual Health, she dedicates a whole chapter to this.

She says,

> Make a list of what is most important to you. . . .
> I might challenge you a bit when I suggest that
> priorities are not what we state them to be but
> how we're actually spending our time. We can't
> give lip service to one thing and say it's a
> priority if we are spending our time doing
> something else. Obviously, what we're
> spending our time doing is what we have
> established as our priorities.

My list of priorities would be family, home, friends, myself, writing, Northern Colorado Writers, volunteering, and reading. Notice, obsessively checking email, watching *Downton Abbey*, perusing Facebook, and alphabetizing my spice rack is not on my priority list, but these are things I waste my time on. Clearly I can cut these activities out and open up more time to writing. Pretty easy choice.

Some choices, though, are not so easy. My writing buddy Laura made some huge cuts this year. She has been a stay-at-home mom and freelance writer/radio commentator for years, but decided she was not reaching her full potential as a writer, so she did something about it.

She declared to her family and friends that writing was now her job. The hours while her kids were at school would be her official work time. That was the easy part. The tough part came when she had to decide what to cut out of her day to make this happen. It meant no more weekly volunteering at school, no more breakfasts out with friends, and no more shopping trips during the day.

One of her biggest challenges was getting her friends and family to accept this. When a friend would call to see if Laura could do lunch, she would have to decline because she was working. Or if her daughter called because she forgot her lunch, Laura would have to tell her to charge a lunch because she was working.

This wasn't easy for her, but she stuck to her guns and is feeling good about her decision. Plus she is getting a bunch of writing done.

Are you ready to reach your full potential as a writer? If so, what are you willing to cut out of your life in order to do that?

NOVEMBER

"You can fix anything but a blank page."
—Nora Roberts

Writing Goals for the Month

_____

_____

_____

_____

_____

Action Steps to Achieve Your Goals

_____

_____

_____

_____

_____

Reward

_____

FOLLOW YOUR NOSE

-Jenny

Much (sometimes too much) is made of the fact that we have a two-party political system in this country, but we tend to be either/or people in many other ways, too. Coffee or tea? Boxers or briefs? Cats or dogs?

My answer to that last one is dogs, and I'm not alone. My dog is one of nearly 80 million canine companions in this country. We have birthday parties for them, take them on vacation with us, and put their faces on t-shirts and coffee mugs. Naturally, our love of dogs is reflected in our reading material, as evidenced by the many recent dog-themed best-sellers, from *Marley* to *Sawtelle* to *Racing in the Rain*. In *I Thought You Were Dead,* author Pete Nelson even gives Stella, an aging German Shepherd/Labrador mix, the ability to carry on regular conversations with her owner, Paul.

I sometimes wish my dog could talk because I'd love to have a better understanding of how she perceives the world. I know that her powers of observation are much sharper than mine. She sees things I don't see, hears things I don't hear, and the nose factor—well, that's not even close. Humans have approximately 5 million sense receptors for olfaction. Bloodhounds have 300 million. Dogs can sniff out bombs, drugs, lost hikers, cancer, and, of all things, whale feces. I suspect my dog can smell when I'm just thinking about bacon.

Now, don't get me wrong, I'm not exactly envious of the ability to track down a sweaty sock from a mile away. But I do think I'm a better writer when I'm in tune with my senses—and that seems like it's getting harder to do. We humans are chronically distracted, and so much of what we take in is already neatly formatted and packaged for us. We are told what we are experiencing and often don't think about the nuances we are missing.

How might my writing be different if I took a lesson from my dog and followed my nose more often? Well, I might sniff out a great idea for a story or character. I might also stick my nose somewhere it doesn't belong, but all writers should (safely) do that from time to time.

As for my dog's conversational abilities . . . perhaps she would be less like Stella, who speaks in proper sentences ("Lunch was delicious, Paul. Thank you very much for that special treat.") and more like the grammar-challenged pooches who grace the front of greeting cards. (I can haz a treet now?) It wouldn't matter. I'd still want her as my coauthor.

But a cat would make a better editor, don't you think?

THANKFULNESS

-Kerrie

As we get closer to Thanksgiving, most of us put more thought and energy into recognizing what we are thankful for. Family, friends, our home, our health—these are the things that surface quickly. But what about things related to your writing? What are you thankful for in that realm?

I know this might seem crazy to some people, but what about editors and agents? Their job can't be an easy one—wading through queries and proposals from people who never read the guidelines, editorial meetings, emails, talking with agents, working with authors/writers, and then actually editing.

We spend a lot of time trying to figure out what they want. We send them queries and proposals and then a lot of times deal with the rejections that follow. But when one sees the merit in our idea, our book, our poem, and they want to publish our work, it is a great feeling.

Forming a good working relationship with agents and editors is what every writer should strive for. Then when you have another idea for an article or a book, the door is already open (which we all know is the most difficult part of the business, getting that door to open). It is also imperative to continue working on that relationship. If you are working with a magazine editor, continue sending her ideas so that she knows you are serious about your writing. If it is a book editor, be sure to be working on your next project while polishing the first one. Then when the first book is done, you have another one ready to pitch.

Regardless of what type of editor/agent you are working with, stay professional and pleasant. Keep phone calls and emails to a minimum. Be someone you would like to work with.

Back to the idea of thankfulness. One thing I try to do once a year is take some time to thank the editors I have worked with over the past year. I send them a card and usually some small/inexpensive gift. Those in the publishing world work hard, and I bet they rarely get acknowledged for it. I do this because I want them to know how much I appreciate their hard work and to thank them for believing in my writing.

I challenge you to take some time this month to acknowledge those editors and agents you have a working relationship with. If you are not there yet, take some time to thank those who are helping you try to get there (your spouse, your writing group, a writing buddy). Just take some time out to show your gratitude.

Whom can you thank this week?

MONET'S VISION

-Jenny

I'm one of those lucky people who have needed to wear glasses since, well, conception, considering my genes. Growing up, my annual eye exam invariably resulted in thicker lenses, which is why I dread the eye doctor the way some people dread the dentist. And now that I'm reaching a certain age, I'm having more trouble seeing up close. Truly, we lifelong myopes—who squint at the swimming pool, battle with foreign matter under our contacts, and have had a lens restriction on every one of our driver's licenses—should be spared the additional hassle of presbyopia.

(Yes, I know about Lasik, but I'm a total chicken.)

But as anyone with more significant visual impairments than mine could attest to, vision is not always synonymous with eyesight. Dictionary.com defines vision as "the act or power of sensing with the eyes," "the act or power of anticipating that which will or may come to be," and "a vivid, imaginative conception or anticipation." That last one is my favorite.

Painters, photographers, and the like depend heavily on eyesight. I find it interesting that many famous visual artists endured eye troubles. Claude Monet and Mary Cassatt had cataracts. Camille

Pissarro had a malfunctioning tear duct. Edgar Degas suffered from what was probably macular degeneration. These artists continued to paint as long as they were able, and consequently their work reflects both their eyesight and their creative vision. In Monet's case, some of his most famous works were painted when his cataracts were at their worst.

I can barely draw a bath, so I primarily use words as my medium. In fiction, we do our best to visualize entire novels from beginning to end, including characters and plots and settings that may be completely unique to our own internal landscape. And we all, from the most minimalist poet to the most epic fantasy author, must also see our own writer's journey—where we've been, where we are, where we're headed.

I've recently been to the eye doctor, so I know how my eyesight is doing. (More of the same, but thanks for asking.) But it has been quite a while since I've examined my writer's vision. Am I proceeding from a place of "a vivid, imaginative conception or anticipation?" Or am I becoming increasingly short-sighted? Maybe it's time I tweaked that prescription, too.

How's your writer's vision doing these days?

THANKFUL FOR WHAT DIDN'T HAPPEN

-Kerrie

On this day before Thanksgiving there are lots of great blog posts floating around on the Internet about being thankful for what we have. Like these bloggers, I am very thankful for all the wonderful blessings in my life. But, on the flip side, there are some things I am thankful that never happened:

- I am thankful I didn't get my first children's book, *Candy Corns and Lollipops*, published.

- I am thankful I didn't get torn into a million little pieces by Oprah on national television like James Frey did.

- I am thankful I didn't listen to some of the suggestions and critiques of my writing.

- I am thankful I didn't let my shyness get in the way of meeting new people at writers conferences and events.

- I am thankful I didn't let a few "no thank yous" by publishers and editors stop me in my quest to get published.

What are you thankful that you DIDN'T get?

WRITE WHAT YOU KNOW
-Kerrie

Write what you know. This is a mantra repeated over and over again in writing circles. Taken at face value, this could sound like a limiting statement, but the truth is, it opens the world up to you.

In a recent class with narrative nonfiction author Greg Campbell, he agreed that you should write *what you know*. But he added, "The best ideas come from going out into the world and turning over rocks." You should be constantly expanding your experiences to add more to your *what I know* repertoire. By doing this, it adds depth and texture to your writing that might not have been there otherwise.

For his book *Blood Diamonds*, which was a prime reference for the movie with Leonardo DiCaprio, he did more than research the diamond trade in South Africa through the Internet and phone calls. He actually went there. He learned firsthand about the culture, the diamond trade, and even tried to buy and smuggle a diamond from the black market.

For his book *Flawless*, which is about the largest diamond heist in history, he and his coauthor went to Amsterdam where the robbery took place. They visited the places and talked to the people who were key players in this heist. So when it came time for him to write, he could include details and elements in the story that he would not have been able to if he had not been there.

This works for fiction as well. YA author Laura Resau does this brilliantly in her book *The Indigo Notebook*. Resau has lived and traveled extensively in Latin America, and she uses these experiences in her fiction.

There is a scene in the book where she describes a marketplace in Otavalo, Ecuador:

> Soon I turn a corner, and there it is, Plaza de Ponchos, a sea of tarps and tables spread with fuzzy scarves and sweaters and bags, flower-embroidered shirts, sparkly silver jewelry, woven rugs, heaps and heaps of colors spilling out everywhere.

Resau could have gotten this info from a photo, but this next part clearly comes from her experiences and adds a texture to the writing that could not have been captured from a picture.

I weave through the tunnels of stalls that smell of wool fresh off llamas and sheep and alpaca, an earthy animal smell mixing with the exhaust of passing cars. Tourists are chatting with vendors, reaching out to test the itchiness level of a poncho, or holding up a brown sweater beside a gray sweater to decide which color looks best. Meanwhile, the vendors are cajoling in singsong voices, a mix of Spanish and heavily accented English.

Through her detailed descriptions, Resau is able to paint a sensory picture for her readers that establishes a strong sense of place. It immerses them in the story and allows them to be more connected to the places, events, and characters.

Keep in mind that you don't have to travel around the world to expand *what you know*. Keep your eyes and ears open to what is happening around you. Don't be afraid to talk to people and learn more about them. Ask questions. Listen. Learn.

Campbell had a great story about having a couple of young LDS men show up at his door. Rather than turn them away like he usually did, he invited them in to talk. He wasn't interested in becoming a Mormon, but he wanted to learn more about these two young men and why they did what they did. Now he has a new experience and new knowledge he can draw from in the future.

Do you write what you know? What lengths have you gone to in order to experience something you wanted to write about?

DECEMBER

"Either write something worth reading or do
something worth writing."
—*Benjamin Franklin*

Writing Goals for the Month

_____

_____

_____

_____

_____

Action Steps to Achieve Your Goals

_____

_____

_____

_____

_____

Reward

_____

MAKING SENSE OF IT ALL
-Kerrie

A few years back I had the privilege of hearing Chris Ransick speak at a luncheon. After hearing him read some of his work, it was obvious to me why Chris was Denver's Poet Laureate. He talked all about the importance of engaging our readers through the five senses, because it is through our senses that we experience life and give meaning to it.

Imagine if you close your eyes and someone holds a fresh-cut orange under your nose. You inhale the sweet, citrus aroma and then your brain combines the smell with your life experiences and tells you that it is an orange you are smelling. It is through our senses we live our lives, so why not include them in our writing as well?

I always knew how important it was to include the five senses in my writing. After hearing Chris, I started paying more attention to my sensory experiences in my everyday life and how I could connect them to my writing. I found that the more senses I used, the more engaged I was in the experience.

Yesterday, I decided to get out my Christmas decorations and don the house in holiday splendor. After dragging all the plastic tubs out of the dusty crawl space, I put on my Christmas music, lit a pine-scented candle, and poured myself a glass of freshly chilled Pinot Grigio. As I began unpacking all the treasures, the smell of pine started filling up the air, I started singing along with the Christmas songs, and with each item I took out, wonderful memories of Christmases past flooded my mind.

When it was all done and I sat down to relax, I truly understood what Chris was talking about. As I decorated the house, I was completely engaged in the moment. I wasn't thinking about bills that had to be paid, articles that were due in a couple of days, the laundry, all the presents I still needed to buy—all of that had disappeared.

We need to do the same thing with our writing—whether you write fiction, nonfiction, poetry, whatever, you must engage your reader through their senses, the more the better, without forcing it. If the reader is completely engrossed in what s/he is reading, the rest of the world temporarily fades away for them. They are completely engaged. You have now created an experience for them, not just a piece of writing. And people remember experiences.

Next time you sit down to write, activate some of your senses before diving in. Light a candle, get a cup of tea, put on some music, then start writing. By being in the moment and enjoying the experience, you will be able to pass on those feelings to your readers.

Which of the five senses do you tend to ignore in your writing?

ALL THAT JAZZ
–*JENNY*

I have a favorite jazz station I like to listen to when I'm in the car, and not long ago one of the DJs mentioned how jazz is uniquely American music, which moved up from its birthplace in New Orleans to the clubs of Chicago and New York. It didn't take long before the classic New Orleans sound, such as King Oliver's Creole Jazz Band, inspired other musicians, from Duke Ellington to George Gershwin to violinist Paul Whiteman, and widened the scope of the music's popularity.

But the Jazz Age was about much more than music. It was the era of flappers, Prohibition, Al Capone, and Charles Lindbergh. And, musicians aside, perhaps no one embraced the spirit of the times more than the writers: Sinclair Lewis, Edna St. Vincent Millay, Eugene O'Neill, Langston Hughes, Dorothy Parker . . . and, of course, F. Scott Fitzgerald, who is credited with coining the term "Jazz Age."

Fitzgerald was only 24 in 1920 when his first novel, *This Side of Paradise*, made him famous overnight. (Imagine that, right?) Feeling that he could then support a wife, he married the beautiful Zelda Sayre, and the two lived and chronicled the excesses and cynicism of the era. From Scott's "Commentary on New York" (1926):

> The restlessness approached hysteria. . . . Young people wore out early—they were hard and languid at twenty-one. . . . The city was bloated, glutted, stupid with cake and circuses.

We all know that soundtracks are an integral part of a moviegoing experience, but books can have soundtracks, too. Take this quote from *The Great Gatsby*:

> All night the saxophones wailed the hopeless comment of the Beale Street Blues while a hundred pairs of golden and silver slippers shuffled the shining dust.

Just as with movies, the soundtrack of a book is best if it conveys mood without overpowering plot or characters. Above all, it has to "sound" right.

The Roaring Twenties, of course, was not the only era to be shaped by its music. Rock and roll in the fifties, disco in the seventies, grunge in the nineties—each of those musical styles, and many more, can be a powerful tool for anchoring a character in a particular time, setting, or mood.

Think of songs you love—or hate—and write them below. Then build characters around those songs.

PRIORITIES
-Kerrie

A few years ago, I had a bad fall and ended up completely dislocating my shoulder. Because my shoulder was out for so long (about four hours), there was a lot of soreness, pain, and numb fingers. It took about four weeks before I regained full use of a few fingers, making typing nearly impossible.

If you have had something sudden happen in your life like an accident, illness, or challenge, you will understand what I am talking about when I say that priorities shoot to the surface and everything else seems to falls away. I knew I had to figure out who was going to get my kids back and forth from school for a few days, check to see if I had any deadlines coming up, and cancel any appointments that could wait.

All of those other little things—dusting, sorting through my files, putting holiday decorations in every nook and cranny of my house, and making my house spotless for an upcoming party—didn't seem as important anymore. My family was taken care of, and I was taking care of myself. The rest of the things would have to wait, or, as with the house, my standards would have to drop from spotless to merely clean.

My mind usually races with all the little things I have to do. The truth is, when my mind was relaxed and going at a slower pace, the world did not fall apart. I could actually think more clearly.

Obviously, the accident forced me to slow down. I couldn't continue at this pace forever. But it made me think that there must be a compromise. There must be a way to prioritize life through our words and actions and still be successful, relaxed, and happy.

Many people, including me, will say they have certain priorities, but when you watch how they live their lives, it contradicts what they say. I wonder if it is because we have too many priorities on our list— or what we think are priorities, anyway.

Maybe our true priorities are those things that are at the core of who we are. Our beliefs, the things that make us tick, the important people in our lives . . . the things we can't live without.

For many of us, the need to write is at our core. We feel drawn to it; it gnaws at us. It is a true priority for us, but our actions don't always show that. We put the writing on a special shelf and only take it down on special occasions or when we feel worthy enough. We forget about it with all those small day-to-day activities that might not be in line with our priorities.

Below, make a list or think about the top seven priorities in your life.

1. _____
2. _____
3. _____
4. _____
5. _____
6. _____
7. _____

Are you living your life supporting those priorities? Do you need to make some changes? Do you need to let some of the smaller stuff fall away? What can you do to line up your priorities with how you live your life?

A NEW SLANT

-Kerrie

At church this past Sunday the pastor mentioned that for the past 23 years he has looked forward to the challenge of coming up with a different message and creating a new slant on the very familiar Christmas story.

It made me start thinking of my own freelance writing and how the biggest challenge at times is coming up with a new slant to an idea. I teach in my magazine writing classes that there really aren't any new ideas, there are just new ways to present the ideas.

You would think editors are tired of getting articles about dieting, but every January, the cover lines at the newsstands seem to all be about losing weight. Other "evergreen" topics are money, politics, family, sex, food, and travel. You can always create articles related to these subjects. Right now "going green" and the economy are hot topics. If you can take an idea and give it a green or economic slant, I imagine you would sell a lot of articles.

My point to all of this is that if you are a freelance writer, all the ideas for your soon-to-be articles are already out there, you just have to find a new or not-done-recently slant. At times it feels as though everything has already been done, but I assure you it hasn't. If a pastor can come up with 23 different ways to present the Christmas story, I think we as freelancers can come up with some new takes on old ideas and make some sales in the upcoming year.

What are some old ideas that you can rethink and make new?

THE TORTOISE OR THE HARE

-*Jenny*

Christmas is approaching, and I'm pretty sure one of my favorite gifts will be a new (nonliving) turtle. A while back, my younger son decided that I should collect them, and he should be the one to give them to me. The third I received from him is a stone pendant he found at one of our favorite local nature shops. The other day when I put it on, I realized that turtles and writers share some important traits:

We're patient with a less-than-speedy pace. Writing can be slow. Revising can be slow. Editing can be slow. When the polishing is finally done, the submission process can be the slowest part of all. Thanks to email, some industry folks are quite quick these days—I once received a "no thank you" to an electronic query in the time it took for me to grab a "congratulations-I-sent-it" cookie (which then became a consolation cookie). But many others still take weeks, if not months, to reply, which can test the most steadfast resolve.

We're persistent. I've read that the jaws of snapping turtles sometimes don't unlock even after death. Although this does evoke the unsettling image of me sitting at my desk in full rigor mortis with a copy of the *Writer's Market* clamped in my hands, writers are well-served by that kind of persistence. Grab onto your dream, and don't let go for anything.

We have thick shells. Even the personal, encouraging rejections sting a little. And the others ... well, if you've been there, you know what I mean. A hard carapace is very useful for ego protection.

Turtles have been on this planet for 230 million years—ages longer than Euripides, Shakespeare, and Ray Bradbury combined. As one might expect from such ancient residents, turtles and tortoises figure prominently in myth and folklore from all over the world. They are generally seen as creatures of endurance, strength, longevity, fertility, wisdom, and perseverance. These are all qualities I gladly embrace as a writer.

I do have days when I wish my career would leap, hare-like, from the starting line. But for now, I'll just keep moving steadily forward. And if I take some chances by sticking my neck out from time to time, I may find I was closer to my goal than I thought.

As a writer, are you a turtle or a bunny?

Shepherding Our Writing

-Kerrie

At church recently, the pastor was talking to us about the shepherds in the Christmas story: how they were going about their usual shepherding tasks when all of a sudden an angel appeared and changed their lives forever:

> Luke 10And the angel said unto them, Fear not: for, behold, I bring you good tidings of great joy, which shall be to all people.11For unto you is born this day in the city of David a Saviour, which is Christ the Lord.

After hearing the message and getting over the initial shock of what just happened, they decided to set out on a journey to Bethlehem to see for themselves what the angel was talking about. The pastor went on to illustrate how we can learn from the shepherds and relate this to our lives today and of course it made me think of writing. Here are the three points he shared. We must learn to

1. Face our fears.

For the shepherds, this meant dealing with angels popping up out of nowhere. As writers, our fears are the blank page/screen, rejection of our writing by editors/agents, and harsh judgment of our work. But if we let these fears paralyze us, we will never find what we are looking for.

2. Determine what it is we are looking for.

The shepherds knew they were heading to Bethlehem to find a baby wrapped in swaddling clothes, lying in a manger. They had direction and purpose. As writers we too must figure out what we are looking for. Is it publication? Writing a best-seller? Sharing information about a cause regardless of the pay? Making a living as a freelancer? Writing a memoir for family members? Whatever the goal is, if we don't figure out what it is, we end up frustrated and lost because we have no direction.

3. Be people of action.

The shepherds did not sit around and talk about how great it would be if they went to find the baby. They got up and did it. I come across so many people who talk about wanting to write, but that is as far as they get—talking about it. Being a writer means you have to do one thing and that is write. Whether you set aside 30 minutes a day or few hours a day it doesn't matter, you just have to take action and put pen to paper or fingers to keyboard.

Do you know what you are looking for with your writing?

THE GREATEST GIFT
-*Kerrie*

As we approach Christmas, the hectic holiday life amps up a notch. Thoughts of decorations, parties, and gifts fill our brains. We become consumed by it all.

I am not saying it is bad thing. I personally love the holiday season. But I do catch myself at times getting a little too caught up in it all, while I run around trying to find the perfect gifts for family, friends, teachers, neighbors. It seems during all this hustle and bustle, the one person I forget about is me.

There is one gift you can give yourself that is more valuable than anything else and it won't cost you a cent. How about honoring yourself with the gift of time? This time can be used to work on your novel, send out queries, journal—basically it is time to just write.

To make this more fun, write down on a small certificate the days and times you are giving to yourself. Wrap it up and open it on Christmas (or another holiday if you don't celebrate Christmas). After you open it, write the info in your daytimer and hang up the certificate. Don't waste the gift.

Respect yourself and your writing enough to keep these times and enjoy doing it.

How much time are you going to gift to yourself?

*Another page intentionally left blank for
Notes and Doodles*

WRITER'S BLOCK CURES

Photos: Use a photo to spark an idea for a setting, character, article, storyline…

~Pick one of these photos, study it for one minute and then write for 10 minutes about it.

Get Creative

~Do artsy-craftsy activities (scrapbooking, collages, woodworking, etc.) that spark your creativity and stimulate your brain.

Concrete Poem

~A concrete poem is a shape poem where the words relate to the topic while forming shape/s to illustrate the poem's subject. In the space below, create a concrete poem about a **flower, mountain** or **fire.**

~Dig out your kids' cast-off art supplies. Draw a picture. If it's hard for you, all the better. Writing is so much easier than drawing a realistic giraffe.

~Draw doodles all over this page.

Go Outside

~Walk. Outside. With your dog, if you have one. Leave the iPod and earbuds at home. Look around. Don't think about writing. Just watch and listen. Breathe.

~Go find a place to sit outside. Get comfortable, then close your eyes. Focus on your breathing and the sounds around you. Do this until all the thoughts vying for your attention get quiet and all you are thinking about is the symphony of sounds surrounding you.

Step Away From Your Computer

~Give your hands something to do that doesn't take much concentration. Wash dishes, clean windows, sort through the sock drawer. Save the open-heart surgery or laser calibration for later. Let your mind wander.

~Go to a bookshelf—yours, the library's, a bookstore's. Pull off a book at random, open it up, and read a few passages. Repeat as many times as necessary. Be sure to put the books back or you may be asked to leave. Even by your spouse.

~Turn on the TV. Find the most mindless, unappealing programming you can. Force yourself to watch until you can't stand to waste another moment of your precious writing time with such drivel.

~Get out paper and a pencil/pen. Set a timer for ten minutes. Write nonstop about something other than your work in progress. Grocery lists, vacation plans, lines from Dr. Seuss, the beginning of a short story that goes nowhere, it doesn't matter. Just keep writing.

~Get a camera/phone and take pictures (Either inside or outside). Play around with the point of view. Get close for some shots. Try different angles. Experiment with the composition (things don't always have to be centered). Do this for at least 15 minutes. Take a few minutes to look over the photos.

~Put on classical music (yes, classical). Then find a comfortable place to relax. Close your eyes, listen and imagine the music is the background for a scene in a movie. Enjoy what unfolds.

Write a letter. Get out some stationary or create your own stationary and write a letter to a friend or family member you haven't spoken to in a while. Then send it out.

TOOLS

Essential References for Your Bookshelf

Writer's Market, Robert Brewer

100 Words Almost Everyone Confuses & Misuses

Flip Dictionary, Barbara Ann Kipfer

The Elements of Style, Strunk & White

The First Five Pages, Noah Lukeman

The Emotion Thesaurus, Ackerman & Puglisi

Save the Cat, Blake Snyder

Formatting & Submitting Your Manuscript, Chuck Sambuchino

The Writer's Journey, Christopher Vogler

Guide to Literary Agents, Chuck Sambuchino

Inspirational

On Writing Well, William Zinsser

Walking on Water, Madeleine L'Engle

On Writing, Stephen King

Bird by Bird, Anne Lamott

The Right to Write, Julia Cameron

Madeleine L'Engle Herself: Reflections on a Writing Life

Chicken Soup for the Writers Soul, Bud Gardner

The Artist's Way, Julia Cameron

Handy Websites

Random name generator
http://www.behindthename.com/random/

Preditors and Editors
http://pred-ed.com/

Writer's Beware
http://www.sfwa.org/other-resources/for-authors/writer-beware

Media Bistro
https://www.mediabistro.com/

Funds for Writers
http://www.fundsforwriters.com/

Wow! Women on Writing
http://www.wow-womenonwriting.com/

Evernote
https://evernote.com/

Pomodoro Technique
http://pomodorotechnique.com/

Scrivener
http://www.literatureandlatte.com/scrivener.php

Writing Conferences

Of course, our favorite conference is the Northern Colorado Writer's Conference, since we help organize the event. Every year we bring in agents, editors and writing experts from all over the country to our wonderful city, located at the base of the Rocky Mountains. In order to provide the highest level of personal experience for each participant the conference attendance is limited to 130 writers.
http://www.NorthernColoradoWriters.com

Websites with lists of others Writer's Conferences:

New Pages
http://www.newpages.com/writing-conferences/

Shaw Guides
http://writing.shawguides.com/

Writing Contest Links

Northern Colorado Writers Contests
http://northerncoloradowriters.com/upcoming-events-mainmenu-133/writing-contests

Poets and Writers
http://www.pw.org/grants

Writer's Digest
http://www.writersdigest.com/competitions/writing-competitions

New Pages
http://www.newpages.com/classifieds/writingcontests/

For Fun

Virtual Poetry Magnets
http://magneticpoetry.com/pages/play-online

Language is a Virus
Great website with lots of fun writing activities
http://www.languageisavirus.com/

Every Photo Tells a Story
http://everyphototellsastory.blogspot.com/

Track the submissions you send out through the year on the following pages.

Submission Tracker

Item Sent Out_____

Date_____   Publication_____

Person Sent to_____

Email or Address_____

Response_____

Follow up_____

Item Sent Out_____

Date_____   Publication_____

Person Sent to_____

Email or Address_____

Response_____

Follow up_____

Item Sent Out_____

Date_____   Publication_____

Person Sent to_____

Email or Address_____

Response_____

Follow up_____

Submission Tracker

Item Sent Out_____

Date_____ Publication_____

Person Sent to_____

Email or Address_____

Response_____

Follow up_____

Item Sent Out_____

Date_____ Publication_____

Person Sent to_____

Email or Address_____

Response_____

Follow up_____

Item Sent Out_____

Date_____ Publication_____

Person Sent to_____

Email or Address_____

Response_____

Follow up_____

Submission Tracker

Item Sent Out_____

Date_____   Publication_____

Person Sent to_____

Email or Address_____

Response_____

Follow up_____

Item Sent Out_____

Date_____   Publication_____

Person Sent to_____

Email or Address_____

Response_____

Follow up_____

Item Sent Out_____

Date_____   Publication_____

Person Sent to_____

Email or Address_____

Response_____

Follow up_____

Submission Tracker

Item Sent Out_____

Date_____   Publication_____

Person Sent to_____

Email or Address_____

Response_____

Follow up_____

Item Sent Out_____

Date_____   Publication_____

Person Sent to_____

Email or Address_____

Response_____

Follow up_____

Item Sent Out_____

Date_____   Publication_____

Person Sent to_____

Email or Address_____

Response_____

Follow up_____

KERRIE FLANAGAN

Kerrie Flanagan is the Director of Northern Colorado Writers, an accomplished freelance writer and a writing consultant. Her articles have appeared in the 2011 Guide to Literary Agents, as well as the 2012, 2013 and the 2014 Writer's Markets, Writer's Digest Magazine and The Writer.

She was a frequent contributor for WOW! Women on Writing and enjoyed two years as a contributing editor for Journey magazine. Five of her stories are found in various Chicken Soup for The Soul books. Her book, *Planes, Trains and Chuck & Eddie*, made its debut at the end of 2013.

Her background in teaching and her passion for helping writers reach their full potential led her to form Northern Colorado Writers in 2007. This group supports and encourages writers of all levels and genres.

When she is not writing, Kerrie enjoys fly fishing, sharing a good bottle of wine with friends, going to the movies and camping with her family. She loves hot tea (especially jasmine), even when it is 90 degrees outside.
http://www.KerrieFlanagan.com
http://www.NorthernColoradoWriters.com

JENNY SUNDSTEDT

Jenny Sundstedt is pleased to be the co-author of *Write Away: A Year of Musings and Motivations for Writers.* Much of her life has been spent making up stories, and after earning a degree in Anthropology and working such diverse jobs as shoe seller, computer chip fabricator, and legal assistant, she decided it was time to start writing stuff down. Despite constantly looking for the next great thing to procrastinate, she has two fiction manuscripts (and counting), several short stories, and many blog posts under her belt. She assumes that's why her jeans feel a little snug.

Years of writing and being a stay-at-home-mom may have exacerbated her innate hermit-like tendencies, but she can still be found out in the open on occasion, taking pictures, having fun with her family and dogs, and thinking up a compelling backstory for the person ahead of her in line at the deli counter.

She is very grateful to be a part of the wonderful community of Northern Colorado Writers. She would also like to thank the Pulitzer Prize committee. Someday. She really would.

OTHER

HOT CHOCOLATE PRESS BOOKS

Planes, Trains and Chuck & Eddie

A Lighthearted Look at Families

https://www.createspace.com/45 13167

And Then I Smiled

Reflections on a Life Not Yet Complete

https://www.createspace.com/ 4644658

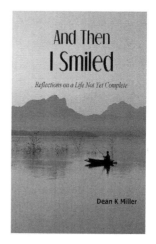

Made in the USA
San Bernardino, CA
27 May 2014